BEST RADIO
PLAYS OF 1980

BEST RADIO
PLAYS OF 1980

The Giles Cooper Award Winners

Stewart Parker: The Kamikaze Ground Staff Reunion Dinner
Martyn Read: Waving to a Train
Peter Redgrove: Martyr of the Hives
William Trevor: Beyond the Pale

EYRE METHUEN/BBC PUBLICATIONS

First published in Great Britain in 1981 by Eyre Methuen Ltd
11 New Fetter Lane, London EC4P 4EE and BBC Publications,
35 Marylebone High Street, London W1M 4AA.

Set in IBM 10pt Journal by 𝑻\ Tek-Art, Croydon, Surrey
Printed in Great Britain by Richard Clay (The Chaucer Press) Ltd,
Bungay, Suffolk

ISBN 0 413 48600 1

CONTENTS

THE GILES COOPER AWARDS: a note on the selection

Giles Cooper

As one of the most original and inventive radio playwrights of the post-war years, Giles Cooper was the author that came most clearly to mind when the BBC and Eyre Methuen were in search of a name when first setting up their jointly sponsored radio drama awards in 1978. Particularly so, as the aim of the awards is precisely to encourage original radio writing by both new and established authors — encouragement in the form both of public acclaim and of publication of their work in book form.

Eligibility

Eligible for the awards was every original radio play first broadcast by the BBC domestic service from December 1979 to December 1980 (almost 500 plays in total). Excluded from consideration were translations, adaptations and dramatised 'features'. In order to ensure that the broad range of radio playwrighting was represented, the judges divided the awards according to length, while also looking for variety in subject matter and technique. Plays were chosen from each of three categories: those over an hour long; those over 30 minutes but no longer than 60; and those of 30 minutes or less.

Selection

The producers-in-charge of the various drama 'slots' were each asked to put forward about five or six plays for the judges' consideration. This resulted in a 'shot-list' of some 30 plays from which the final selection was made. The judges were entitled to nominate further plays for consideration provided they were eligible. Selection was made on the strength of the script rather than of the production, since it was felt that the awards were primarily for *writing* and that production could unduly enhance or detract from the merits of the original script.

Judges

The judges for the 1980 awards were:

Martin Esslin, Professor of Drama, Stanford University, California and ex-head of BBC Radio Drama

Nicholas Hern, Drama Editor, Eyre Methuen

Dickon Reed, Acting Script Editor, BBC Radio Drama

Gillian Reynolds, radio critic, *The Daily Telegraph*

THE KAMIKAZE GROUND STAFF REUNION DINNER

by Stewart Parker

Stewart Parker comes from Belfast and is currently living in Edinburgh. He has been, at various times, a university teacher in America, a local broadcaster in Ulster, and the rock music correspondent of the *Irish Times*. His first radio play was broadcast in 1967 and there have been five or six more since then, including *Minnie Maisie and Lily Freed* and *The Iceberg*. His stage and television plays include *Spokesong*. (Evening Standard Most Promising Playwright Award, 1976), *I'm a Dreamer Montreal* (Christopher Ewart-Biggs Memorial Prize, 1979), *Catchpenny Twist*, *Kingdom Come*, *The Actress and the Bishop*, *Nightshade*, and *Iris in the Traffic, Ruby in the Rain*.

The Kamikaze Ground Staff Reunion Dinner was first broadcast on BBC Radio 3 on 16th December 1979. The cast was as follows:

MAKOTO	John Le Mesurier
TOKKOTAI	Ronald Baddilley
CO-PILOT	John Sheddon
AIR TRAFFIC CONTROL	John Sheddon
SHUSHIN	Graham Crowden
MISS TOMISHITA	Maureen Beattie
SHIMPU	Ronald Herdman
KAMIWASHI	Harry Towb

Director: Robert Cooper

Sound effects: fade up dentist's surgery.

MAKOTO. Wide as you can, please. Good. Mina, hand me the . . . whatsiname. Thanks.

The clink of dental instruments.

Dear oh dear, look at this. Swollen gums . . . nicotine stains, chipped edges. A right little den of iniquity, that's what we've got here (*The patient grunts.*) Mina, hand me the . . . pronged thingy. Now, then. Let's have a good probe. Yes . . . these teeth have certainly seen some heavy action . . . not from a toothbrush either. (*The patient grunts.*) Now, chewing gum, yes . . . cigarettes. Confectionery. Not to mention bean paste pickles for lunch, eh? (*The patient exclaims with pain.*) Sorry . . . cotton wool, Mina . . . thanks. Yes . . . what I'll have to do on this little monster . . . is a bit of a root canal procedure . . . no time for that today, I'm afraid . . . you'll need to come back in the morning. (*The patient grunts.*) Still, there's a few quickies here I can wrap up now. Nothing to worry about. A bit wider . . . good.

Drilling.

Any other day, you see . . . I might stay on late . . . but I have a dinner engagement tonight. Mina, have you got the, uh . . . thanks. Yes, I've got a date with my old war-time cronies this evening . . . of the Imperial Japanese Naval Air Arm. As was. Actually, you might be more comfortable with an injection . . . Mina? . . . thanks. Yes, there's rather more to this little horror than I thought . . . we were all stationed at Mabalacat Base in the Phillipines together, you see. Open wide . . . good . . . yes, with the Special Attack Force . . . you know, the Kamikazes . . . (*The patient shrieks.*) Easy . . .

Crossfade to hissing drone of engines in the cockpit of a jet airliner.

TOKKOTAI (*suave and soothing*). Hello Ladies and Gentlemen, this is Captain Tokkotai speaking again. Sorry about the continuing delay.

We do expect to be cleared for landing at Tokyo very shortly, since we have been in a holding pattern now for some forty-five minutes. It appears that student disturbances in the airport buildings are once again the cause of this unfortunate hold-up. However, the situation should clear quite soon and I'll keep you posted. Thank you.

He switches off the cabin P.A.

(*In his normal voice.*) . . . you mob of overbearing ignoramuses.

CO-PILOT. Mostly cockeyed with drink by now, I should imagine.

TOKKOTAI. All whining and snivelling and browbeating the poor bloody cabin staff.

Crackling on radio.

AIR TRAFFIC CONTROL (*distorted gibberish*). Zulu Delta QNH one zero one five over.

TOKKOTAI. What? What was that?

CO-PILOT. Not for us, I don't think.

TOKKOTAI. I can't understand a word they say any more. I mean, you'd think they'd have Air Traffic Control who could at least speak plain Japanese. They're all aborigines from Hokkaido or somewhere . . . . all inbred. They've all got cleft palates and hare lips and loose dentures.

CO-PILOT. I don't believe that left fuel gauge.

TOKKOTAI. Why should you, this whole machine's a piece of ramshackle junk, I've seen cattle wagons better built . . .

AIR TRAFFIC CONTROL (*as before*). Papa Charlie maintain hold and stand by please over.

TOKKOTAI. What? Did you catch that?

CO-PILOT. Just saying stand by, I think.

TOKKOTAI. Half of them are foreigners, you know. Bloody Koreans and Fillipinos and Chinks from Taiwan. They just walk through Immigration and straight into jobs in the Control Tower. They read everything out of a phrase-book, strictly mumbo-jumbo.

CO-PILOT. Shouldn't we be banking now?

TOKKOTAI. All right, all right . . . going round in bloody circles . . . I just wish they'd let me loose among those Commie students . . . with a machete and a machine gun, that's the kind of education they're in need of . . .

CO-PILOT. That gas temperature's fishy as well.

TOKKOTAI. I mean, here we are slaving like pigs, paying out a ransom in taxes so they can go to university . . . and they're down there, running round in helmets with big sticks, beating up the riot police and setting fire to the airport.

CO-PILOT. Well, that's their crusade in life. Just like the war was for you.

TOKKOTAI. The war? You're not seriously comparing the nation's greatest sacrifice with the hooliganism of a molly-coddled rabble of subversive degenerates?

CO-PILOT. Well, not in so many words . . . but there again . . .

TOKKOTAI. Unbelievable!

CO-PILOT. Blood pressure . . .

TOKKOTAI. It's thanks to those pigs that I'm liable to miss my reunion dinner tonight . . . with the men I was proud to serve beside in the war.

CO-PILOT. Really? It was the Naval Air Force, wasn't it?

TOKKOTAI. Damn right. Although not as pilots, not then. We were maintenance engineers, as it happens. (*Slight pause.*) As a matter of fact, we were the men who serviced the Kamikaze Corps, I suppose you find that amusing?

CO-PILOT. Not just at the moment, no.

(*Crossfade drone of engines with dentist's drill. Drill stops*).

MAKOTO. Right. A little rinse out, please.

The patient slurping mouth-rinse, swilling it round.

Of course you realise this particular tooth is actually dead. The nerve's dead. It can still continue in service, though — I'll sort of plug it for you.

The patient spitting out and clearing his throat.

Okay, let's drop in. (*He chuckles.*) That was our private slang, you know. That's what we used to call the suicide missions . . . dropping in. Gallows humour, I suppose. Mina, could you hook on that . . . you know, contraption?

Gurgling of saliva vacuum.

Thanks. Yes . . . we were the blokes who put the planes in the air. Kept them airworthy. It was a bit of an about-turn at first. One day, you see . . . you're working hard to make sure the plane can get back to base. Next day you're making sure it's fit enough to drop in. The big thing was — don't let the pilot down. There he is, sitting in the cockpit . . . in his rising-sun headband. He's said his goodbyes . . . made his peace with the world . . . drunk the ceremonial cup of saké. The engines are revving . . . his comrades are lining up for take off . . . he runs the final checks . . . and his joystick comes right off in his hand. Well, you can imagine our mortification at that sort of eventuality. All set to gas yourself and the meter runs out kind of thing . . . funny, this stuff doesn't seem to be drying very quickly, Mina . . . honestly, the suppliers these days, you never know what they're sending you . . . oh, well. (*A pause as he works on.*) No, our job was to get them safely up in the air and safely over the target so they could crash on schedule. Now, just bite down hard on that . . . good. The work was a real killer, but you'd never hear anybody complaining. Pulling together for the country . . . that was the style then. Rather infra-dig these days, of course. (*Pause.*) What a terrific gang too . . . the ground crew at Mabalacat, I mean. Tubby Tokkotai . . . Shorty Shushin . . . Tokkotai's a pilot now, oddly enough. (*The patient grunts.*) Yes, that looks to be a sensitive spot . . . Old Shushin runs a little bakery.

A door is knocked on.

MISS TOMISHITA. It's only me.

SHUSHIN. Yes?

The door opens;

Ah, come in, Miss Tomishita.

MISS TOMISHITA. Output figures for the week, Mr Shushin.

SHUSHIN. Oh, dear. Yet another nose-dive, I suppose?

MISS TOMISHITA. 'Fraid so. It's like they always say on the radio — this work-to-rule's really beginning to bite . . . especially among the cream buns! (*She whoops with laughter.*) Oh, Lord, you have to laugh don't you?

SHUSHIN (*sadly*). And what has been the worst hit this week, Miss Tomishita?

MISS TOMISHITA. Well now, let's see . . . the French bread, the Swiss rolls, the Danish pastries, the English muffins and the Gipsy creams.

SHUSHIN. All our main lines, in fact.

MISS TOMISHITA. The pumpernickel's up to quota.

SHUSHIN. It's no good . . . we're losing orders in all directions. Two more weeks of this and we shall be facing liquidation.

MISS TOMISHITA. There there, Mr Shushin — never say die. That's what I always say.

SHUSHIN. It's a phrase I myself never use now — not since the dreadful day when I said it inadvertently to a kamikaze pilot.

MISS TOMISHITA. Never say die . . . (*she whoops.*) . . . oh lord, you do have to laugh.

SHUSHIN. He was just about to take off on his heroic mission. 'Shushin,' he said to me, 'I was going to ask you to post a letter for me' — they often would do that — 'but', he said, 'I've gone and neglected to procure a stamp for it.' 'That's all right, sir,' I said, 'I have a stamp, never say die.'

MISS TOMISHITA. I'm sure he had a giggle at that.

SHUSHIN. It was not a giggling matter, Miss Tomishita, I really wished the ground would open up and swallow me. But he pretended not to notice my appalling gaffe — they were like that, you see. Perfect gentlemen. He just handed over the letter with a cheerful smile. It was addressed to his mother.

MISS TOMISHITA. Couldn't you just cry your eyes out . . .

SHUSHIN. And then off he flew.

MISS TOMISHITA. To hurl his handsome young body against the advancing enemy ships.

SHUSHIN. And six hours later he was back.

MISS TOMISHITA. Back?

SHUSHIN. They couldn't find the target. That often happened, you know, especially in bad weather. Made it all the worse, of course, for me.

MISS TOMISHITA. As well as his poor mother.

SHUSHIN. Pardon?

MISS TOMISHITA. The letter. Thinking he was killed.

SHUSHIN. Oh, no, I hadn't posted the letter. We never did that till we knew for certain the mission had succeeded. I gave it back to him.

MISS TOMISHITA. Imagine him having to suffer through that whole ordeal again.

SHUSHIN. In his case fate strangely intervened, Miss Tomishita. On his way to the mess hall that evening he was run over by a motor-cycle dispatch rider. By the time he was able to walk again, the war was over. (*With gravity*.) And that man today, Miss Tomishita, is a Senior Vice President at the Yoshimitsu Electronics.

MISS TOMISHITA. Get away.

SHUSHIN. Picture my chagrin to find him the guest speaker at a management conference in Osaka only last year.

MISS TOMISHITA. No.

SHUSHIN. I did my utmost to keep out of his sight, of course. But at the reception I suddenly found that we were standing side by side in the Gents.

MISS TOMISHITA. You surely must have jogged his memory.

SHUSHIN. It wasn't my place to speak to him, so I just stared at the wall, though I could sense him looking me over. But he never said anything. Perhaps he just failed to recall my face after thirty-five years.

MISS TOMISHITA. He knew you rightly, Mr Shushin, but he probably wants to forget about the whole terrible business.

SHUSHIN. I shouldn't think he could forget, Miss Tomishita. I know I certainly couldn't forget those years. They were the happiest years I ever spent.

Crossfade to the interior of the jet cockpit.

TOKKOTAI (*to the radio*). Papa Charlie willco. Confirm QFE 1005 over. (*Pause.*) If those young fighter pilots could see what has happened to this country since the war ended . . .

CO-PILOT. I'm glad they didn't divert us, at least.

TOKKOTAI. Look, you can see them now, swarming round Terminal 3 like vermin.

CO-PILOT. Who, the passengers?

TOKKOTAI. The so-called student demonstrators. Vicious little buggers. Look at them. (*To the radio.*) Papa Charlie established over.

AIR TRAFFIC CONTROL (*as before*). Roger.

TOKKOTAI. And you, Jack. (*Pause.*) I'd really love to smash this whole jerry-built contraption right into the middle . . .

CO-PILOT. Listen, I can finish taking her down if you feel like a rest or whatever.

TOKKOTAI. I'm not entirely senile yet, you know.

CO-PILOT. Just a trifle tired, I shouldn't wonder, what with the delay and the cross winds and what not.

TOKKOTAI. Listen, sonny, I didn't get the scrambled egg on my cap in exchange for Green Shield stamps.

A faint whining noise starts.

CO-PILOT. Of course not, chief.

TOKKOTAI. I am the pilot. I will land the plane. What's that noise?

CO-PILOT. Cabin pressure warning, I think.

TOKKOTAI. See if you can switch it off, it's distracting,

The noise stops.

CO-PILOT. It stopped by itself.

TOKKOTAI. Fouled up, like everything else. (*Pause.*) You're too young, you see, you don't know what this country was like when the people still believed in it. As a nation. Before they sold out to the yen. That's all anybody believes in today, the almighty yen, that's why we're ruled over by a cartel of shady businessmen, a crowd of crooks and swindlers, that's the example set to the nation by our illustrious leaders. But you take a man like Admiral Ugaki, now. I suppose you've never even heard of him?

CO-PILOT. I think I remember you mentioning him once or twice before.

TOKKOTAI. There was a man who didn't measure human beings in terms of the yen. He measured them by their actions. And he put his money where his mouth was.

CO-PILOT. Hara-kiri, wasn't it?

TOKKOTAI. Better than that, sonny. (*To the radio.*) Papa Charlie outer marker over.

AIR TRAFFIC CONTROL. Roger.

TOKKOTAI. We're talking about a man whose orders had dispatched countless young pilots on their death missions, right? So come August 15th, 1945. The Yanks have dropped their A-bombs. The Emperor has broadcast the Surrender Rescript. The war's over, right? Ugaki's in charge of the naval air base on Kyushu. He issues orders to prepare the remaining few Ohkas for flight. I don't suppose you even know what an Ohka is, well it's not something you'd want to fly, sonny, I can assure you of that. It was a one-ton bomb with a pilot on top and a crude rocket in its arse. It was carried to the target dangling from a Ginga bomber and then released. Strictly a one-way ticket. (*To the radio.*) Papa Charlie lights in sight over.

AIR TRAFFIC CONTROL. Roger.

TOKKOTAI. There were these steps cut into the cliff overlooking Sasebo Bay. They led down to a plank runway we'd got hidden in the sand. No sooner had we the planes trundled out and the warheads primed than Ugaki appears at the top of the steps, in full dress uniform, holding a samurai sword, and his fellow officers behind him. Then it finally dawned on all of us. They were going to personally fly the final kamikaze mission of all. So we stood to attention as they came down the cliff steps and Ugaki marched right up to the Ohka which I had personally serviced. He handed me the sword to hold while he climbed in, and then he took it and laid it between his feet and gave the order for take off. And I don't mind telling you, sonny, that I was with him in spirit as he headed out over the Pacific. Just try to visualise it . . . dropped from the Ginga twenty-five miles from Okinawa . . . firing the rockets, roaring towards the bay at 600 miles an hour, gaining speed as he dives through the flak . . . picking out the flight deck of the fattest carrier in the harbour, steering your nose right at it . . .

CO-PILOT. We're too low, oh my God, a bus . . . missed it by a whisker!

Wheels crunching on the runway, engines going into reverse thrust.

TOKKOTAI. There we go, home at last, and about bloody time too. Fancy a beer, old man?

Crossfade scream of engines with atmosphere of dental surgery.

MAKOTO. Listening to the talk of those pilots . . . you couldn't believe how cool they were. You'd hear one say to the other, something like . . . Hey, what about aiming for a funnel? Those funnels are very lightly armoured. And the other fellow would say, casual as you like — yes, but a funnel's curved, it's hard to smash right into it. A final rinse out now, please.

The patient rinsing.

This would be immediately before the sortie, you realise — an hour or two before dropping in.

The patient spits out.

You'd have thought they were discussing a game of snooker or something. (*He chuckles.*) Some men. That feel all right?

The patient grunts.

Fine. Good. That's us all finished for now, then, Mr uh . . . see you tomorrow. Try to avoid eating if you can. Bye-bye now.

The patient goes out. The door closes.

Well, Mina, he didn't have much to say for himself, did he?

Fade out.

SHUSHIN. I just don't understand it, Miss Tomishita. Here we all are in the midst of peace and prosperity. And yet everywhere you look there's resentment and greed and people looking out for their own ends.

MISS TOMISHITA. I'm not hurting your leg, am I, dear?

SHUSHIN. It's just gone to sleep a little.

MISS TOMISHITA. I'll distribute my avoirdupois a bit, then.

The rustle of clothing, scrape of a chair leg.

How's that, dear?

SHUSHIN. Much better, thank you.

MISS TOMISHITA. Just you cuddle up, Mr Shushin, and let's forget all about the stupid work-to-rule for a while.

SHUSHIN. I don't know, all you hear day in day out is differentials, demarcation, incentive bonuses, squabble squabble squabble. There was none of that when we had a war to fight.

MISS TOMISHITA. It brings out the best in people, war.

SHUSHIN. It takes you out of yourself, you see. We never had time to think of ourselves, only of the pilots.

MISS TOMISHITA. And you wouldn't have caught them taking industrial action.

SHUSHIN. Well, you can't down tools at 4.30 when you're flying a kamikaze mission. There's no half measures in war-time, that's the important thing. Everybody gives their all. Nobody gives their all to peace-time, though, that's what I can't understand. They pretend to, but it's very half-hearted underneath.

MISS TOMISHITA. If only we'd won, Mr Shushin, perhaps it might all be different.

SHUSHIN. I don't really think so, Miss Tomishita. I mean, it's not as if our defeat was dishonourable, after all. I always recall the words of Admirable Ohnishi to the Special Attack Corps in Formosa after we had to pull out from Mabalacat. Gentlemen, he said — even if the homeland suffers defeat, it will be saved from ruin. It will be saved by nobility of spirit — the spirit of this kamikaze attack corps — without the spirit of your magnificent gesture, ruin would certainly follow defeat.

MISS TOMISHITA. Beautiful.

SHUSHIN. It will be saved from ruin . . . by nobility of spirit.

MISS TOMISHITA. You say it lovely, Mr Shushin.

SHUSHIN. We were only the humble ground crew, Miss Tomishita, but we shared in that spirit. We had our moments too. You might not believe this — but in one single night we built five Zero fighter planes out of scrap.

MISS TOMISHITA. I'm not keeping you late for your dinner, am I?

SHUSHIN. When I say scrap, of course, I'm referring to old damaged hulks, along with bits and pieces lying around the base.

MISS TOMISHITA. My goodness, it's nearly seven.

SHUSHIN. Seven? Oh dear, I'll need to be getting ready for the reunion.

The sound of clothing and chair as they disentangle and stand up.

It's a big night for me Miss Tomishita.

MISS TOMISHITA. Indeed it is, and I hope you've got a nice clean suit and shirt to change into.

SHUSHIN. Well, as a matter of fact, I took the precaution of changing especially this morning . . .

MISS TOMISHITA (*tut-tutting*). That's shocking, Mr Shushin, attending your regimental reunion in your working clothes.

SHUSHIN. No, no, it's not a regimental . . .

MISS TOMISHITA. You know what you need, don't you? Here, you've got loose threads on that tie . . . hold still . . . there we are . . . what you need is a woman about the house.

SHUSHIN. The 5th of January, 1945, it was.

MISS TOMISHITA. What was that, dear?

SHUSHIN. We received orders to evacuate Mabalacat on that day. All the operational planes had been launched, you see, there were no more left . . . and the American fleet was preparing their final attack. We were supposed to burn all unusable gear and report for duty as ground troops. Well, orders are orders, of course. But we didn't feel like giving up without a parting shot. So we just roamed around the base, scavenging whatever we could find and sticking it together, right through the night. By the next day we had five complete planes more or less in working order, though they wouldn't have passed any regular flight inspection, naturally . . .

MISS TOMISHITA. I expect the pilots were surprised.

SHUSHIN. . . . in fact one of them blew up taking off. There were only thirty pilots left on the base by then and Commander Tamai had asked for five volunteers to fly our Zeros. How many do you think volunteered, Miss Tomishita?

MISS TOMISHITA. I'm quite sure he'd no bother finding five, at any rate.

SHUSHIN. All thirty pilots volunteered.

MISS TOMISHITA. Is that the truth of it?

SHUSHIN. The whole thirty pilots begged for the honour of flying this last mission from Mabalacat.

MISS TOMISHITA. Those were men, Mr Shushin. And the most of them still boys.

SHUSHIN. If only their likes were alive today . . . we'd be a multi-national conglomerate by this time.

MISS TOMISHITA. It plucks the flower of the nation's youth, war. And leaves the weeds to blossom, so it does.

SHUSHIN. Cherry blossom, that was the name they gave to the Ohka bombers. Shed from the young trees. Falling out of the sky in a scattering of terrible beauty.

MISS TOMISHITA. The poet's soul is in you, Mr Shushin. Have you got a clean hanky?

SHUSHIN. I never bother much with hankerchiefs, to tell you the truth . . .

MISS TOMISHITA. Here you are, take mine, I haven't done more than sniff into it. There. That looks very neat in your pocket. You know what you need, don't you? . . .

SHUSHIN. Dear me, look at the time, I'll never find a taxi . . . perhaps you would lock up, Miss Tomishita. (*As he goes:*) Good night, now, see you in the morning!

Fade in taxi interior in the middle of heavy traffic, horns honking.

SHIMPU. Just take a look at these streets. Choking with human garbage . . .

KAMIWASHI. These days there's a policy unique for every case, believe me. Those lights are red, Shimpu.

SHIMPU. This is where my life is lived, driving tourists round the teahouses and drunks round the whorehouses, you really think that's something I want to insure?

KAMIWASHI. It's a point of view, Shimp . . .

SHIMPU. I want to eradicate it!

KAMIWASHI. . . . but there again, think of your dependants, they have got to be provided for, am I right?

SHIMPU. Tell me something, Kamiwashi — how would you describe my wife?

KAMIWASHI. What, sweet little Sayoko?

SHIMPU. Would you say sluggish was the right word?

KAMIWASHI. Plump and cuddly, I'd call her.

SHIMPU. Sluggish. Meaning like a slug. With the sensibility of a slug. And a half-witted slug-like son who earns more as a butcher's boy than I do. What would I want to provide for them, apart from extermination?

KAMIWASHI. Look at the taxi insurance I got you, did it work out good or didn't it?

SHIMPU. It keeps going up, it was one hundred and ninety-seven thousand yen this year.

KAMIWASHI. Purely on account of your unfortunate mishaps, Shimp. The point is, they haven't withdrawn the cover, you're still in business, that's the beauty of that particular firm. Here, that plane's coming in very low. Ooops, careful of the bus.

The sound of the plane passing over. Horns blaring, people yelling.

SHIMPU (*shouting*). You stupid bloody cackhanded gorilla!

KAMIWASHI. That plane nearly clipped his roof.

SHIMPU (*still shouting*). Move your stinking carcass next time!

KAMIWASHI. Look, I'll leave you a copy of the booklet anyway. See, the point is, it's a form of investment. You're still only, what? fifty-four? You were the kid at Mabalacat, right? You've still got a good quarter-century left. At a conservative estimate.

SHIMPU. How can I drive it through your thick skull? Life is already over for me, Kamiwashi, it has been for years. All that concerns me now is the dreary and tedious business of disposing of the remains.

KAMIWASHI. When you're feeling cheerier, though, Shimp, just take a quick little look at this scheme. See, it's index-linked, with an escalator clause, meaning the benefits expand at a royal rate of knots if you only leave it long enough to mature. Say twenty-one years in your case. All you have to do is hang about till you've turned seventy-five and you'll make a killing.

SHIMPU. I have no intention of even reaching fifty-five!

KAMIWASHI. In which case you still clean up on the life insurance, that's the beauty of this plan.

The car begins to move rapidly.

SHIMPU. What the hell do I care if I'm dead?

KAMIWASHI. I use the term 'you', of course, in the sense of your estate.

A barrage of horns.

SHIMPU. I don't have an estate, I have a taxi, a fat wife, a slob of a son, I live like a battery hen . . . there is not a single vestige of beauty in my entire existence.

KAMIWASHI. There's your flower arranging.

SHIMPU. Straight down the incinerator, every time. Broken blossoms . . . I don't have the gift, Kamiwashi. I'm telling you the truth — more and more I realise it — ever since the war ended I've had nothing strong and true and beautiful to live for.

KAMIWASHI. Friendship, Shimpu. You have your friends. You have your old comrades in arms.

SHIMPU. But what are we?

KAMIWASHI. Your band of brothers, Shimp.

SHIMPU. I know, I know . . .

KAMIWASHI. The finest boys you'll ever know.

SHIMPU. What else do you think has kept me going this long? But what are we any more?

KAMIWASHI. You have to admit there's that . . . that sharing, that deep-down sense of . . . of sharing, that bond. You have all that to live for. Those memories . . .

SHIMPU. Memories! Yes! We're only memories, we're no longer flesh and blood, we're just ghosts, do you see?

KAMIWASHI. That bicycle's turning left, Shimp.

The skidding of tyres, horn blaring.

SHIMPU. All we've got in common is our losses. Don't you see that? Our lost youth . . . our lost war . . . lost ideals, lost country . . .

KAMIWASHI. Wrong, Shimpu, wrong. We've got everything to cherish — the memories, the ideals. All to be cherished. So maybe we're not youngsters anymore, but that's just where good insurance, for instance, comes to our aid . . .

SHIMPU. Don't start on bloody insurance again!

KAMIWASHI. Merely an example. Just to make the point. We're all family men now — aside from old Shushin — we're providing for our families, we're all doing very nicely, face it. Tokkotai's a pilot — flying high — Makoto's coining money as a dentist, lucky devil — I just fixed him up with a loan for a second car, as it happens. Shushin's running a bakery, with a generous slice of crumpet under the counter, thank you very much and good evening. You're in business for yourself, driving your own hack. And yours truly — otherwise known as Kamiwashi Financial Services Inc. — is assisting one and all to maximise their assets. And here we are again, all set to guzzle a few bones, snort a cup of saké, and Bobo's your uncle.

The car begins to slow down.

So cheer up, my old friend, cheer up. (*A brief pause.*) What are you slowing down for?

SHIMPU. We've arrived.

KAMIWASHI. God Almighty, so we have.

Sound effects: after-dinner chatter in a hotel function room. Then tapping on a water glass, chatter subsiding.

TOKKOTAI. Gentlemen — warriors of old — as on previous occasions it is my pleasant duty to preside over our little reunion — and to start the round of toasts on its way. (*Murmurs of 'Hear, hear' etc.*) Our company has somewhat dwindled in numbers over the years — though I think I detect several new chins in attendance this year — (*Laughter.*) but no matter — they haven't got the better of us yet, by God — nor will they, so long as we keep alive the old Special Attack Force spirit!

Defiant cries of assent, and thumping on the table.

Gentlemen — you don't need me to tell you how that spirit has been all but extinguished in modern Japan . . . a point I had occasion to make to my co-pilot only this afternoon . . . in fact, my very presence here tonight was put in jeopardy by the infantile vandalism of a gang of state-subsidised Communist delinquents!

KAMIWASHI. Not another speeding fine, Tubby?

Laughter from the others.

TOKKOTAI. I shall ignore that cheap jibe. I am going to invite you now to raise your glasses to the memory of a man whom I know you all revere. I refer of course to the late Admiral Takijiro Ohnishi. Let me recall for you the words he spoke to the twenty-four pilots of the very first Special Attack Corps — those immortal words that we were privileged to hear and can never forget. 'Japan is in grave danger. Her salvation lies beyond the power of ministers of state and the General Staff, let alone that of humble commanders like myself. Only you the vanguard of young warriors can save her. On behalf of your hundred million countrymen, I am asking you for this greatest of all sacrifices, and I pray for your success. You are already Gods beyond earthly desires.' (*Pause.*) Admiral Ohnishi, my friends.

They all repeat the toast and drink.

SHIMPU (*choking back a sob*). He had such dignity!

TOKKOTAI. Oh God, is that little fairy starting already?

KAMIWASHI. Drink up, Shimp. (*To* TOKKOTAI:) He's been under a bit of strain lately.

The background chatter has meanwhile resumed.

MAKOTO. How's the gingivitis problem these days, Shimpu?

SHIMPU. I don't know, I never think about it.

MAKOTO. That's all very well, but it won't go away without treatment.

SHIMPU. You think I care? I like it. I like having the taste of blood in my mouth all the time. It strengthens my resolve.

MAKOTO. You won't like it when your teeth start falling out.

SHIMPU. Let them! What's the odds . . . my whole mouth can putrefy like a rotten fruit, so far as I'm concerned, along with everything else.

MAKOTO. Mind you, it's going to take a fair course of treatment to fix you up. What you need, you see, is a bit of a gingivectomy procedure, and then we could fit you up with a good firm set of dentures.

SHIMPU. My God, dentures . . . was there ever a word with less poetry in it, was there ever a term more ugly and disgusting?

MAKOTO. It's not half as disgusting as the state of your gums.

SHIMPU. Listen, Makoto, I know you all think I'm something of a joke, no, don't bother denying it — as a matter of fact, I feel like something of a joke — but just tell me, aren't you occasionally overcome with disgust at it all yourself?

MAKOTO. Of course.

SHIMPU. Don't you ever feel an impulse to cry out in protest, to smash it all right into the ground?

MAKOTO. Certainly — every time I look into somebody's mouth.

Tapping on a water glass. The background chatter subsides.

TOKKOTAI. Mr Shushin has the floor.

SHUSHIN. Oh. Thank you, Tokkotai.

MAKOTO. Hear, hear — a toast from the baker.

KAMIWASHI. Never mind the toast, Shushin, what about the crumpet, eh?

Laughter from the others.

SHUSHIN. Pardon?

KAMIWASHI. No buns in the oven, I trust?

Laughter.

Tapping on a water glass.

TOKKOTAI. Order, if you please.

SHUSHIN *(clearing his throat)*. Thank you. Gentlemen — more and more often in these days of difficult industrial relations . . .

MAKOTO *(sotto voce)*. I'm bored already.

Shushing from the others.

SHUSHIN. . . . one casts one's mind back with a certain regret . . . to . our days together in the Naval Air Arm.

TOKKOTAI. Send the whisky up, somebody.

SHUSHIN. United as we were then by a common purpose . . .

KAMIWASHI. . . . removing Fillipino knickers . . .

Suppressed sniggers, shushing.

SHUSHIN. . . . officers and men worked in harmony as one. I think in particular tonight of the high regard in which we all held Commander Nakajima . . .

TOKKOTAI. Hear, hear . . .

SHUSKIN. . . . and I remember that never-to-be-forgotten occasion . . .

KAMIWASHI *(sotto voce)*. . . . which has momentarily slipped my mind . . .

Suppressed sniggers.

SHUSHIN. . . . em, that occasion upon which he gathered together the whole ground crew . . . to thank us for our splendid work . . . and upon which he advised us occasionally to relax.

SHIMPU. } To which you had the honour of replying . . .
MAKOTO. }

SHUSHIN. To which it fell to me . . . em, to have the honour to reply
. . . 'Thank you, sir, but we can always nap in the shade of our planes'
wings . . . whenever there is nothing needing to be done'.

Dutiful/ironic applause.

SHIMPU (*sotto voce*). Arse-licking as usual.

SHUSHIN. Therefore, gentlemen . . . I offer the toast . . . of Commander
Nakajima.

They all repeat the toast and drink. Fade out.

Background chatter more animated.

KAMIWASHI. See, I ask myself, Shushin — what is the root cause of
your problem, right?

SHUSHIN. It's the unions, that's all.

KAMIWASHI. And speaking in a nutshell — the root cause can be
summarised as an unhappy work-force, am I right or wrong?

SHUSHIN. They never even have the good grace to say 'Good morning'
to me now.

KAMIWASHI. So what we have to ask ourselves is — what is the source
of, or root cause of this discontentedness, this malaise of the
employees? Where might it originate?

SHUSHIN. They want more money but they won't work for it.

KAMIWASHI. Benefits, Shushin. Ever think of benefits, eh? Pension
scheme, superannuation? Life insurance, health insurance — for the
whole family? Low-interest loans?

SHUSHIN. They've got all that.

KAMIWASHI. Comparability, Shushin. That's the point. How do your
benefits compare with those of rival bakeries?

SHUSHIN. Well, of course, the big conglomerates . . .

KAMIWASHI. The big conglomerates, exactly. They can offer so much
more . . . half a dozen free loaves a week . . . annual sex excursions
to Bangkok . . .

SHUSHIN. Did I ever tell you about my long week-end in Manila?

KAMIWASHI. See, what your benefits need, Shushin, is a thorough
going-over. Now, I guarantee that I could update your whole system
of benefits — at a very small cost to the firm — to the point where
your work-force would be begging you on their bended for extra
overtime.

Tapping on a water-glass. Chatter subsides.

TOKKOTAI. Order, order. I now call on Mr Makoto.

SHUSHIN. Yes, order for the dentist, now.

Cheers, whistles, getting quite drunken.

MAKOTO. Gentlemen — in the course of my daily work, I have at various times given some of you the needle (*Laughter.*) — bored the teeth off others (*More laughter.*) and put the rest to sleep (*Much laughter.*) but I assure you that I plan to refrain from doing any such things this evening.

Applause, cry of 'Sit down then'.

I cannot tell you how much more pleasant it is — to look at your familiar faces grouped around a table — fat and flushed and sweaty as they are — (*Cry of 'Watch it' etc.*) — than to see them tilted back in my chair — eyes rolling and mouth wide, like a cow about to be shot in the abbatoir. You can't imagine how much more tolerable you are when your mouths are shut.

KAMIWASHI. And we feel the same about you, Makoto, right men?

Cries of assent.

MAKOTO. But of course, some familiar faces are not grouped round this table, though they should be . . . some mouths are shut forever . . . those of our comrades who died at Mabalacat or subsequently. And so, let's drink to them, gentlemen: to our departed friends.

They repeat the toast, 'Departed friends' and drink.

SHIMPU (*breaking down again*). I wish to God I was with them.

TOKKOTAI. Oh shut up, you little pansy.

MAKOTO. Steady on the throttle, Tokkotai.

Background chatter meanwhile resuming.

TOKKOTAI. I'm sick listening to his endless whining and slobbering.

KAMIWASHI. He's a highly-strung lad, our Shimpu, he needs a good cry now and then.

TOKKOTAI. He may have been a lad in 1945, but he's supposed to be an experienced adult by now. That's the kind of spineless snivelling you hear everywhere in this country these days.

MAKOTO. Maybe so . . . but I'll lay you odds . . . if war was declared tonight . . . the young lads of today might surprise you.

TOKKOTAI. It'd surprise me if they could write their names.

MAKOTO. Not that it's likely, another war.

TOKKOTAI. Bloody Yanks put an end to that, didn't they. From now on it's all computers and wizened men in white coats pushing buttons.

MAKOTO. Of course, they do still use bombers.

TOKKOTAI. Except you need a further degree in Physics to fly one.

No, there'll never be another war like ours, Makoto.

Pause.

MAKOTO. If we'd got the A-bomb first, mind you . . .

TOKKOTAI. Not even first! Say we'd had three or four A-bombs . . . just small ones. Even in August, '45 we could have won the whole show with a single kamikaze mission. We could have wiped out the entire U.S. forces with one sortie.

MAKOTO. Makes you wonder how different our lives would be . . .

TOKKOTAI. There'd be discipline! Respect for tradition! None of this tidal wave of Western filth, none of these pimps and embezzlers and second-hand car dealers ruling the roost. The Emperor would still govern, none of this elected representative farce. The heritage of the shogun and the samurai would still prevail. I wish you'd stop hogging the whisky bottle.

MAKOTO. Oh, sorry. There you go.

Sound effect: pouring.

How's Setsuko and the girls these days?

TOKKOTAI. Oh, the usual nagging and bitching and complaining about everything. Never satisfied, women. I've got myself a grandson now, though.

MAKOTO. Have you indeed, nice work. When did this happen?

TOKKOTAI. Just three weeks ago. Here, I think I might have a snapshot somewhere . . . yes, there we are, there's the little blighter.

MAKOTO. He's a sturdy one.

TOKKOTAI. He'll be a fighter. Just like his grandad. It's his christening tomorrow.

MAKOTO. Big day.

TOKKOTAI. You're an old grandfather too, aren't you?

MAKOTO. Oh, yes . . . I've got six at the last head-count. Here, let me show you . . . there they are.

TOKKOTAI. Not all boys?

MAKOTO. Every last one.

TOKKOTAI. You don't know the burden, Makoto, of being the only man in a whole family. Women never off your back. Nowhere to turn for a bit of peace.

MAKOTO. I thought you airline pilots were hardly ever at home.

TOKKOTAI. That's my one salvation. But I'm due to retire in two years. This little blighter's the only ally I'll have then.

The atmosphere is now very drunken.

SHIMPU. Silence! Silence! Listen to me!

Thumping on the table.

TOKKOTAI. Sit down, you horrible little fruitcake.

SHIMPU. I have my toast to make.

KAMIWASHI. Good boy, Shimmy.

SHUSHIN. Yes, let's all have another little toast.

KAMIWASHI. Silence in court, gents.

The din at last subsides a little.

SHIMPU. I raise my glass . . . to the memory of Lieutenant Kuno . . . to his young strong smiling face . . . to the day he thanked me . . .

MAKOTO. For doing what?

SHIMPU. He thanked me . . . because I polished his cockpit.

TOKKOTAI. I'll bet you did.

KAMIWASHI. You were always a great one for the old Vim and Brasso, Shimp.

SHIMPU. Those cockpits were their coffins . . . you wouldn't lay a man to rest in a slovenly coffin . . . that's why I scoured and polished them . . . I know they all appreciated it . . . but he personally thanked me as he warmed up his engine . . . my throat closed over, I couldn't reply . . . all I could do was run alongside as the plane taxied . . . touching his wing tips . . .

KAMIWASHI. Well, here's to him, gents!

Cries of 'Lieutenant Kuno' and a few raspberries blown as they drink.

SHIMPU. Tonight I follow in his glorious wake!

The glass smashes.

Hubbub as SHIMPU *is restrained, crying bitterly.*

SHUSHIN. Oh dear, he seems to have cut himself on the neck.

MAKOTO. It was a knotted scarf in the toilet last year as I recall.

TOKKOTAI. Let him get on with it, for God's sake, give us all peace. Not that he ever intended to.

KAMIWASHI. There, he's calmed down now, haven't you, Shimp? Anybody got an elastoplast?

SHUSHIN. I have a roll of insulating tape.

MAKOTO. That'll do.

SHUSHIN. It's fluorescent.

MAKOTO. Make a pad of his napkin, we can tape it on.

TOKKOTAI. What's all the fuss, I've seen worse scratches from a kitten.

KAMIWASHI. Yeah, but it's bleeding all over his hired suit. They charge you extra for stains.

The sound of tape being pulled off a roll.

TOKKOTAI. God, talk about a pathetic spectacle . . . look at us . . . year in year out the same bloody circus acts, jumping through the same hoops.

KAMIWASHI. Cheer up, Tubby, I'm on next!

SHUSHIN. Come on then, Kamiwashi, tell us a joke.

MAKOTO. Yes, let's have a bit of a giggle.

KAMIWASHI. Well, now, . . . it seems there was one very very skinny colonel in the army, see?

SHUSHIN. This'll be a good one.

KAMIWASHI. Real skin and bone, this chap . . . so anyway . . . after the Surrender was announced . . . all his fellow officers sat down together to commit hara-kiri, right? But he — poor man — just didn't have the guts to go through with it boom-boom!

Laughter and groans from the others.

I thank you . . .

TOKKOTAI. You bloody worm!

SHUSHIN. Is that the end?

TOKKOTAI. How dare you insult the memory of our war heroes with your tasteless sniggering cynicism?

SHUSHIN. Tell us another one.

KAMIWASHI. You heard about the geisha girl and the little green man from Mars?

TOKKOTAI. That's quite enough!

MAKOTO. Oh, let him tell it.

TOKKOTAI. I refuse to sit here and listen to the disgusting vulgarities of a grubby little moneylender!

MAKOTO. Uncalled for, Tokkotai.

KAMIWASHI. No, no . . . Captain Tokkotai's word is law . . . I shall draw a veil over the quip in question . . . and hasten on to a toast.

SHUSHIN. Hear, hear.

KAMIWASHI. Gentlemen — we've all drunk this evening to the

memory of several luminaries — whose names are prominently connected with the First Special Attack Corps. As you all know, I was invalided out from Mabalacat, and later transferred to the Kikisui operations. So here's my toast. To some of the pilots I knew on Kyushu. Whose names you won't have heard of. My friends — to the kamikaze pilots who came home again.

A puzzled buzz.

SHUSHIN. Home again? How could they come home again?

KAMIWASHI. Because they didn't bloody feel like killing themselves and quite right too!

A clamour of protest from the others.

Well . . . all this pious guff and crying into your cups and holier-than-thou . . . let's be honest, even on Mabalacat half the pilots were dead against it.

TOKKOTAI. That is a slander on the heroic dead!

KAMIWASHI. Never mind the heroic dead, they're well taken care of. Spare a thought for the unheroic living, namely us. Come on, Shushin, give us a song.

SHUSHIN. I wish I'd been one of the heroic dead.

MAKOTO. You know, all the time we were wishing to be pilots, they were probably longing to be us.

TOKKOTAI. They freely volunteered to offer their lives for their country!

KAMIWASHI. No on Kyushu, they didn't, not in my time. They were ordered.

A further clamour.

Half of them were only student trainees and reserve ensigns, poor little buggers. One week's indoctrination they got — two days on take off, two days on formation flying and three days target practice — and then off they'd go, like it or not. Talk about suicide pilots . . . they were already half-dead with fright before they'd even cleared the ground. The few who managed to make it safely back again are the real heroes, if you want my opinion.

TOKKOTAI. This is an outrage!

MAKOTO. It might conceivably have gone like that towards the end . . . but you've got to admit it was damned impressive in the earlier days.

KAMIWASHI. Listen, the whole idea was just what old Suzuki called it — a tactic of defeat.

TOKKOTAI. Admiral Suzuki was a traitor to the men who had served under him.

KAMIWASHI. And what's more, the pilots weren't all angels either.

'You are already Gods beyond earthly desires' . . . some of them thought they were Gods all right, but they'd plenty of earthly desires.

SHUSHIN. I wish I'd been a God.

KAMIWASHI. Swanning round the base in their hachimakis — women swooning into their arms. One of them smashed me to the ground once and spat on me . . . just because I'd singed his beautiful eyebrow lighting his Black Sobranie for him.

TOKKOTAI. He should have run you through the gut, you despicable little upstart.

SHUSHIN. They got all the glory. But they couldn't have done anything without us.

KAMIWASHI. Good for you, Shushin old son. You tell 'em.

SHUSHIN. They depended on us, after all. They wouldn't have got too far off the ground without a ground staff to service their engines and patch their fuselage and clear the runways of bomb fragments, and we got strafed and got bombed and kept working flat out, but nobody treated us like earthly Gods and heroic dead.

MAKOTO. Oh, come off it . . . it was just a job, we were only doing our job.

KAMIWASHI. So were they.

TOKKOTAI. Now I've heard everything!

KAMIWASHI. They were professional fighting men. Pledged their lives to the service of the Emperor, am I right? That was their particular line of work. Some did it very effectively, others were fair to middling, and the rest were pretty duff. Now, to take my own case, I sell insurance and the like. That's my line of work. I do it to the best of my ability. I think I do it rather well, on the whole. And as far as I'm concerned, it amounts to much the same thing.

TOKKOTAI. That's the bloody limit, my friend, this charade has gone quite far enough! You were always a cheap and loudmouthed spiv, Kamiwashi, but you've outdone yourself tonight. You sit there in that disgusting Hawaian shirt, smoking a fat cigar, you have the cheek to sit there, stroking your fat paunch with your pudgy fingers, and compare your squalid profiteering with the purest act of selfless courage . . .

KAMIWASHI. Give it a rest, Tubs — you weren't a pilot at Mabalacat, remember, you were just a humble greaser like the rest of us in those days.

TOKKOTAI. You know very well why I wasn't a pilot then.

KAMIWASHI. Yeah, your old man was a window-cleaner . . . and now you've turned into a bigger snob than they used to be back then.

MAKOTO. Uncalled for, Kamiwashi.

TOKKOTAI. You've done your damnedest to deride and defile the historic spirit of the Special Attack Force. You and your verminous kind have done your utmost to trample that spirit underfoot in this country. Well let me tell you that spirit is not dead yet in spite of all your worst efforts, and by God I'm going to demonstrate it to you this very night.

KAMIWASHI. What's he on about now?

TOKKOTAI. If you think flying a kamikaze mission is the equivalent of being an insurance salesman, let's see you do it.

MAKOTO. How can he?

TOKKOTAI. Follow me and I'll show him how.

A puzzled murmur from the others.

For thirty-five years I've watched this country sliding down the drain, and I've been forced to stand idly by. But I thought at least there was still a small oasis of sanity in this particular company. Now I discover that same stench of corruption right here in our midst. Very well. Talk is cheap. Let's see some action.

SHUSHIN. What's he talking about?

KAMIWASHI. His drains are blocked.

TOKKOTAI. Gentlemen, I am proceeding now directly to the airport. Once there I shall commandeer an aircraft, preferably a wide-bodied jet. I shall then fly it up to a height of five thousand feet, and dive-bomb it into the Communist revolutionaries who have seized the Departures Lounge.

Consternation from the others.

Only by such a bold gesture can the soul of Japan be rescued from the ignominy and dishonour into which it has sunk. Like Commander Tamai, I now ask for volunteers to join me in this mission.

SHIMPU. Me! Me! I'll go! I can drive you there in my taxi. Take me, Tokkotai, please, I beg you . . .

TOKKOTAI. All right, all right, calm down for God's sake.

MAKOTO. I don't think you should hit the students. One of them's probably my eldest nephew. Why not do the television tower?

SHUSHIN. Why the television tower?

MAKOTO. Symbolism.

SHIMPU. That's true!

MAKOTO. You could black out those revolting commercials for chocolate-coated peanut butter.

KAMIWASHI. Oh no, my little girls love that stuff.

MAKOTO. They'll be toothless hags before they're thirty.

KAMIWASHI. It's a cute little jingle, though.

SHUSHIN. No, no, that's not the one. What you want to aim for is the Trades Union Federation.

MAKOTO.
SHIMPU. } Oh, rubbish. That's pointless. Makes no sense. Why there?
KAMIWASHI.

SHUSHIN. That's just what they need to bring them to heel. Burn up all their pettifogging rules and their boring negotiations and their interfering in other people's private affairs. Smash right into their big computer!

KAMIWASHI. It's insured for a cool hundred million, that machine. Plus there's the building . . . they'd make a fortune out of it, actually.

MAKOTO. Not if the crash was defined as an act of war, though, surely.

KAMIWASHI. Tell that to the judge, old son . . .

TOKKOTAI. If you've all quite finished — I shall be on my way. The target remains the same.

KAMIWASHI. Come on, Tubs, sit down, it's still early.

TOKKOTAI (*as he goes*). If there are any of you left with guts in your belly, you can follow me to the airport.

SHIMPU (*also leaving*). Wait for me, Captain!

Pause.

MAKOTO. Good God, they've actually gone.

KAMIWASHI. You don't think he's serious?

SHUSHIN. Tokkotai's always serious, that's his big trouble.

KAMIWASHI. Naw . . . he'll come to his senses in the traffic . . . he'll head on home and sleep it off.

Pause.

MAKOTO. Still, we ought to follow them, just in case.

KAMIWASHI. He'll have forgotten all about it by the morning. We don't want to break up the party yet, do we?

MAKOTO. Well, if you feel sure . . .

SHUSHIN. Why don't we all have another little nightcap?

MAKOTO. All right. Good suggestion. Fill them up there Shushin.

Sound effect: pouring.

KAMIWASHI. Oh, come on, we'd better follow them.

Taxi interior in traffic, loud skidding.

TOKKOTAI. Careful man, for God's sake — do you want to get us killed?

SHIMPU. Sorry, Tokkotai.

TOKKOTAI. There's no need to be nervous.

SHIMPU. I'm not, I'm not, I'm just on fire to be there.

TOKKOTAI. You are a warrior now. Remember the Bushido code. You should be calm, watchful. Implacable. (*Pause.*) You should be turning left here.

SHIMPU. No, no, it's faster by the old trunk road.

TOKKOTAI. Nonsense, it's a good two miles further round . . . oh, hang on, I get it. Typical bloody taxi driver's stunt, eh?

SHIMPU. Tokkotai — you know the Yasukuni Shrine?

TOKKOTAI. Of course I know it.

SHIMPU. And you know the old belief — that the souls of the dead heroes all journey there to consort together in eternal fellowship? Do you think our souls will go there?

TOKKOTAI. Who knows. You have to die correctly first.

SHIMPU. I could be with Lieutenant Kuno again for ever.

TOKKOTAI. Listen, Shimpu, when we get to the airport, you stay behind me out of sight. I'll signal to you when I've got things set up.

SHIMPU. What about the others — is there any sign of them?

TOKKOTAI. Can't see a damned thing, the window's so dirty.

Crossfade with a car interior, parked at filling station.

MAKOTO. Fill her up, please. (*To* KAMIWASHI.) Trust me to be out of petrol.

KAMIWASHI. No sweat, we'll soon catch them up in this wagon.

MAKOTO. Only took delivery on Monday. I'd forgotten you had to put petrol in them.

KAMIWASHI. Lovely machine, though.

MAKOTO. You all right back there, Shushin?

SHUSHIN. Must just pop out to the Gents, actually. (*He opens the car door.*) Straight back.

KAMIWASHI. Don't walk around waving the bottle, give it to me.

SHUSHIN. No swigging it all while I'm away, though. (*He closes the car door.*)

MAKOTO. I hope I've got the readies to pay for this . . . hello, look what's in my wallet.

KAMIWASHI. Who's this?

MAKOTO. Tokkotai's grandson. It's his christening tomorrow.

KAMIWASHI. He's the image of his grandad, isn't he. All bald and pouchy-eyed . . . look at that nose too, it's like a pickled beetroot.

The cockpit of a single-engine biplane in flight.

TOKKOTAI. Can't get much height in this crate. Too small and flimsy to cause a lot of damage on impact either. Still, it's the best I could do. Your end okay, number two?

SHIMPU. Yes, thank you, skipper.

TOKKOTAI. Wouldn't let me near the big jets. All the security. All the police and army on account of the building seizure, you see. Should have brought along firearms . . . hijacked a 747. Bit of an oversight on my part, sorry about that. Still. The keys to the old Flying Club came in handy. I'm the President, you see.

SHIMPU. Tokkotai . . .

TOKKOTAI. I'm going to make an approach to the target area from the south-west. That'll keep us out of the airways. Watch out for other aircraft, though. They may send something up to try and force us down.

SHIMPU. Tokkotai, I feel sick.

TOKKOTAI. Also flak. Look out for the flak.

SHIMPU. I'm going to be sick.

TOKKOTAI. What's that?

SHIMPU. Sick!

TOKKOTAI. What do you mean? There's no room to be sick.

SHIMPU. Quick, what'll I do?

TOKKOTAI. Stick your head out here and make it fast!

Sound effects: the cockpit hatch is opened; wind roaring; SHIMPU retching; the hatch is closed again.

You've got it all over your chest.

SHIMPU. I'm sorry.

TOKKOTAI. Clean it off, it's vile.

Crossfade with the interior of a large car moving in traffic. SHUSHIN is singing a selection from 'The Mikado' in the back seat.

KAMIWASHI. Shut up, Shushin.

SHUSHIN. Shush up, Shinshu. (*He giggles, then continues singing softly.*)

MAKOTO. It's got power steering.

KAMIWASHI. And fuel injection.

MAKOTO. Whatever that is.

KAMIWASHI. The executive model, in short. Nifty.

MAKOTO. I've never been any use with mechanical things, you know.

KAMIWASHI. You've come a long way, Makoto.

MAKOTO. I was hopeless with the airplanes. I'm much the same way
    with drills and syringes and things. Yet here I am owning and
    controlling a de luxe automobile.

KAMIWASHI. Well, you're a professional man.

MAKOTO. I look the part, you mean. It's all a matter of behaviour.
    Projecting the image. People are gullible bloody morons, Kamiwashi.

KAMIWASHI. Now there we part company, old son.

MAKOTO. It's all performance, life.

KAMIWASHI. Say what you like, but you didn't get where you are
    without gumption. Without native wit. I didn't get where I am either,
    if it comes to that.

SHUSHIN (*stops singing abruptly*). Where are we anyway?

MAKOTO. Eh?

SHUSHIN. Where are we going to?

MAKOTO. A damned good question, if you ask me.

SHUSHIN. I am asking you. Where's Tokkotai and Shimpu?

KAMIWASHI. God Almighty, I'd forgotten all about them.

MAKOTO. Weren't we meant to pursue them or something?

KAMIWASHI. Never find them now, old son . . .

SHUSHIN. Let's all have another little one for the road. (*He starts
    singing softly again.*)

KAMIWASHI. . . . they'll have passed right through the Departures
    Lounge by this time.

*A brief chortle from KAMIWASHI, then from MAKOTO, which
builds up into helpless mirth from both of them, as SHUSHIN
continues to sing.*

Crossfade with the cockpit of the biplane.

SHIMPU. I feel terrible, all this spinning and dropping.

TOKKOTAI. Shimpu . . . why does it have to be you? Why a pitiful
    sad excuse for a human being like you?

SHIMPU. I'm sorry, I can't help it.

TOKKOTAI. I'd be better off with a babe in arms. Newly born . . . oh Christ. Hold everything.

SHIMPU. I've always been a victim of motion sickness.

TOKKOTAI. Oh, blast. Shimpu, I've just remembered something.

SHIMPU. Even when I was a toddler. Even in taxis.

TOKKOTAI. Look . . . I'm rather afraid there'll have to be a change of plan. I'm very sorry . . . it's highly embarrassing . . . but I've just realised . . . I can't possibly finish the mission tonight.

SHIMPU. Does that mean we're going to land?

TOKKOTAI. The thing is . . . my grandson's being christened tomorrow. Now, I know that may sound as if I'm simply funking it . . .

SHIMPU. I don't care! I just want to lie down somewhere!

TOKKOTAI. I've got to think of my family. It's a question of ensuring the future. He must know in years to come that I was there to name him.

SHIMPU. I think I'm going to be sick again.

TOKKOTAI. Once that's done, the mission can proceed. I give you my word on that. Monday night. All right?

The engine starts to splutter and cuts out.

SHIMPU. What's the matter? What's happening?

TOKKOTAI. Bloody fuel tank. It's registering empty. Could have sworn there was more than that in her.

SHIMPU. What about the reserve?

TOKKOTAI. That was the reserve.

SHIMPU. Oh, my God . . . what'll we do?

TOKKOTAI. Sit tight. No problem. I'll just drift her in for a crash landing.

Sound effects: the hatch is opened; wind roaring; SHIMPU retching.

Sound effects: intercom buzzer.

KAMIWASHI. Yes?

SECRETARY (*on intercom*). A Mr Makoto and a Mr Shushin to see you.

KAMIWASHI. Send them straight in. And if anybody else calls, I'm out for the day.

The door opens.

Morning gents.

SHUSHIN. ⎱
MAKOTO. ⎰ Hello, Kamiwashi. Morning Kamiwashi.

Pause.

KAMIWASHI. Well . . .

MAKOTO. Quite.

SHUSHIN. I still can't believe it.

Pause.

KAMIWASHI. Just madness.

MAKOTO. Maybe. Maybe not.

SHUSHIN. If only I hadn't got so drunk . . .

MAKOTO. We were all drunk.

KAMIWASHI. We can't blame ourselves.

MAKOTO. If I hadn't lost them in the traffic, though . . .

KAMIWASHI. It wasn't your fault. (*Pause.*) These flaming headlines.

MAKOTO. I know.

SHUSHIN. Airline Pilot Goes Beserk. Drunken Joyride Ends In Tragedy.

MAKOTO. Trust them to trivialise it.

SHUSHIN. They all assume it was an accident. (*Pause.*) Maybe we should tell them. Put the record straight.

MAKOTO. Who'd believe it?

KAMIWASHI. Oh, they'd believe it all right. They'd love it to death.

MAKOTO. I don't follow.

KAMIWASHI. Well, you can imagine . . . Wizard Prangs With The Kamikaze Grandads . . . they'd make a right circus out of it.

SHUSHIN. I hadn't thought of it that way.

MAKOTO. You're quite right, though, Kamiwashi.

SHUSHIN. Perhaps we'd best keep mum after all.

KAMIWASHI. No question. Especially if the police get going.

SHUSHIN. Oh, lord . . . do you think they might?

KAMIWASHI. Bound to.

SHUSHIN. If we told them the whole story . . .

KAMIWASHI. No need to.

SHUSHIN. . . . . they could charge us with being accessories.

MAKOTO. I shouldn't think so. Still . . .

SHUSHIN. Mum's the word.

KAMIWASHI. Definitely.

MAKOTO. Yes, that's probably for the best. (*Pause.*) Who could have guessed that they would actually go through with it?

SHUSHIN. They really did have the spirit. The old noble Attack Force spirit. They proved it once and for all. Beyond any doubt.

KAMIWASHI. The question I keep asking myself is . . . why? Why didn't he hit the students in the Departures Lounge as he planned? I mean, why on earth a mobile library van?

Pause.

MAKOTO. Perhaps he simply miscalculated.

SHUSHIN. No, I'm certain it was intentional. A symbolic act. Obviously, when it came to the point, he didn't want to kill other people. Just to make a symbolic gesture. A self-sacrifice.

KAMIWASHI. I don't suppose we'll ever really know, will we?

Pause.

MAKOTO. Still. We ought to make sure it's not forgotten. At least not amongst those few who know the truth of it.

SHUSHIN. What I thought was — how about some sort of memorial dinner in their honour? Just for those who knew them really well?

KAMIWASHI. You know, I think if Shimp and Tubby were here, they'd really appreciate that.

MAKOTO. We could also raise some cash that way to help out Shimpu's wife.

KAMIWASHI. If only he'd bought that policy off me yesterday afternoon . . . (*Pause.*) Lord . . . what a way to go, eh?

MAKOTO. Dropping in . . . out of the sky . . .

SHUSHIN. . . . both eyes glued on the target . . . throttle open wide . . . not a flinch . . . not a blink . . .

MAKOTO (*softly*). Banzai!

WAVING TO A TRAIN

by Martyn Read

For C.B.R.

Martyn Read was born in Henley-on-Thames in 1944, and was educated at Lord Williams' Grammar School, Thame. After thirteen jobs in six years (including grape-picking in Spain, estate agent, tractor-driver and potboy in an Oxford college) he became an actor, and has worked extensively in theatre, radio and television, most recently in the BBC series *Flesh and Blood*. He has written a great deal of revue and cabaret material (co-writing the Radio 4 comedy series *A Little Night Exposure*) and over a hundred songs, many of which have been broadcast. *Waving to a Train* is his second play for radio. He lives in North London, likes gardening, snooker, playing the piano, watching cricket and listening to radio.

Waving to a Train was first broadcast on BBC Radio 4 on 25th November 1980. The cast was as follows:

MOTHER	forty-six	Diana Bishop
SUSAN	fifteen	Elizabeth Lindsay
RICHARD	eight	Jill Lidstone
RICHARD	as a grown man	Michael Jayston

Director: David Spenser

*Fade up full sound effects of the English summer countryside, as lush
as possible, to be held under throughout the play. In the distance we
hear voices, gradually approaching, though they never reach full volume.*

RICHARD. Hurry up, you two! Only to the top of this hill.

MOTHER. Coming as quick as we can.

SUSAN. Are we nearly there, Mummy?

MOTHER. Nearly there. Over the stile.

SUSAN. We've come miles.

RICHARD (*calling*). Slow coaches. Beaten you!

SUSAN. I'm tired.

MOTHER. Now buck up, Susan dear.

RICHARD. She's always tired.

SUSAN. Oh shut up you.

MOTHER. Now we're all going to have a lovely time — is that understood? On we go then.

RICHARD (*man*). A summer day, late in June 1953. The kind of day
that exists only in memory. A burning blue sky, a heat haze
shimmering, almost tangible. Deep fields, quiet fences, flowers,
butterflies, bees, skylarks — and a new Queen crowned. The full
rich cornucopia of summer. On such days . . . On such days, the
three of us, Mother, Susan and myself would walk. Walk for miles.
Along lanes, over streams, through fields; carrying an old army
groundsheet to sit on and a picnic packed carefully into the green
shopping bag. Always there was a small purpose to the expedition;
a visit to a tiny secret church, stone-cool inside; sometimes a
particular tree with huge gentle branches. But best I remember a
day such as today when our destination was no more than the brow

of a little hill. Running hard, the grass stinging my legs, I always reached the top before the others. There I sank to my knees and gazed transfixed down the embankment on the other side. At the bottom, glinting endlessly in either direction, lay a single railway track. Today was special. Today at the top of the bank I had a terrible excitement in my eyes and a fear in my stomach I didn't understand. For today, we would be waving to a train.

MOTHER. Richard, not too near the edge, dear.

RICHARD. Will it be here soon, Mum, will it?

MOTHER. You're not to sit on the grass Richard. You'll catch a chill. And then you'll be sorry.

RICHARD (*quiet*). I've never caught a chill.

MOTHER. Come along, Susan. We're waiting for the groundsheet.

RICHARD. *Mum* — what time will the train come?

MOTHER. In God's good time, dear. Susan, I shan't ask you again.

RICHARD (*quiet*). But what time is *that*?

SUSAN. Why do we have to come all this way to watch a stupid train?

MOTHER. Just help me spread the groundsheet . . .

SUSAN. We always do what he wants.

MOTHER. Now you know that isn't true dear. We take turns to choose. It's very fair.

SUSAN. It isn't.

MOTHER. No sulking, my girl, or you shan't come again.

RICHARD. Good. She always spoils it.

SUSAN. But it *isn't* fair. And don't you see? I don't *want* to come for walks anymore.

MOTHER. Oh? And what would milady prefer to do?

SUSAN. Well, why can't I go down the town sometimes and sit in the café with my friends?

MOTHER. Susan, how often do I have to say it? The British Restaurant is not a nice place for a young lady to be seen in.

SUSAN. Oh Mum . . .

MOTHER. I simply do not want you to associate with the people who go there. Rude, common people.

SUSAN. But all my friends are allowed to go. Avril calls me stuck up.

MOTHER. Sticks and stones can break my bones, but names can never hurt me.

SUSAN (*quietly*). That just isn't true . . .

MOTHER. No more argument now. I won't have the day spoiled. And keep your hat on. The sun is very hot. Richard do come and sit down. The train won't come any sooner for your wishing it.

RICHARD. I thought I could see the smoke.

MOTHER. Don't be silly dear. I'll tell you when it's time. Now come and rest — we've had a long walk.

RICHARD. Oh all right . . . (*He approaches.*)

MOTHER. Move over Susan.

RICHARD. Mum . . .

MOTHER. Mmm?

RICHARD. D'you think the Queen's ever been in a train?

SUSAN. Course she has, stupid.

RICHARD. Didn't ask you.

MOTHER. Now you two. The Queen has her own special train dear. The Royal Train.

RICHARD. Her own train? Cor.

SUSAN (*beat*). Mum d'you think we can watch Mrs Brain's television set again soon?

MOTHER. We must wait to be asked, dear. After all, she did let us watch the whole of the Coronation.

SUSAN. Do you remember the King being crowned when you were young?

MOTHER. Of course I do. May 1937. Just a month or so before I was . . . Before your father and I . . .

RICHARD. Why did I have to wear a black tie when the King died?

MOTHER. A mark of respect, dear. You always wear black when someone . . . someone dear to you dies.

RICHARD. Did you, when Daddy . . .

MOTHER. My goodness, this isn't very cheerful is it? Let's enjoy the weather, shall we? Stretch out and rest. Mmmm. Oh what a beautiful day. So warm and still. As though the world doesn't exist anywhere else. If only . . .

RICHARD (*man*). Yes, if only . . . I know what you're thinking. But he's gone. Seven years gone. A letter from his C/O; a War Office telegram. 'Regret to inform . . .'

MOTHER. Don't; please . . .

RICHARD (*man*). And in exchange you received an illuminated scroll from the King. It used to hang in the drawing-room: 'Held in honour . . . Gave his life to save Mankind from Tyranny.' A fighter pilot, crashing into flames? A spy refusing to talk? No. Just an amiable middle-aged man, an army clerk who gently faded away in a foreign land, in 1946. When it was all over . . .

MOTHER. But . . . God has his reasons.

RICHARD (*man*). And you still believe in that God, don't you? You were hurt and bewildered. But you never ceased to trust.

MOTHER. I *have* to trust. Because . . . when I die, I'll see your father again. And it will be eternity. Don't take that from me, please.

RICHARD (*man*). A terrible God, a vengeful God . . .

MOTHER. Don't say such things. Plenty of women would envy me. I have my children. I am a lucky woman.

RICHARD (*man*). A lucky woman, lying now in the June heat in a loose print frock patterned with big bright flowers, her white arms never red from the sun. Susan, fifteen years old in red gingham check, no longer at ease being a child. Myself, eight, nearly nine, in Aertex shirt and cotton shorts. Restless. All three in sunhats and sandals. A curious little trio. Waiting.

MOTHER. Mmmm. Isn't this nice?

SUSAN. Yes . . .

RICHARD. Mmm. Mum, I read in a book that if you put your ear to the railway line, you can hear the train miles before you see it. I could try that, couldn't I, Mum?

MOTHER. You most certainly could not. I never heard of such a thing.

SUSAN. Mummy, you know that lady with the blue hair who keeps The King's Arms?

MOTHER (*guarded: she disapproves*). What about her?

SUSAN. They say the man who lives there isn't really her husband.

MOTHER. Susan!

SUSAN. They say her real husband put his head on the railway track before the war. Is it true, Mum?

MOTHER. I'm shocked. Who on earth told you such a thing?

SUSAN. My friend Avril. She knows everything.

MOTHER. That girl. I do wish you'd choose your friends with a little more care.

SUSAN. It is true, though, isn't it?

MOTHER. You're not to listen to idle gossip.

SUSAN (*with quiet satisfaction*). I knew it was.

RICHARD. Perhaps he was listening for a train.

MOTHER. Don't be silly, Richard.

RICHARD. *My* friend Norman says if you put two halfpennies on a railway line and a train goes over them, they stick together and make a penny.

SUSAN. Stupid waste of money.

RICHARD. Could I try that Mum? I'd be ever so careful and it wouldn't take long.

MOTHER. Richard, it is very dangerous to play on a railway line. Besides, it's private property. What do you think the fence is for?

SUSAN. My friend Avril says rules are made to be broken.

MOTHER. On the contrary, rules are made to be obeyed. And we've heard quite enough from your friend Avril. Now just close your eyes and rest. Both of you.

RICHARD. And then can we have the picnic?

MOTHER (*yawning*). We'll see, dear, we'll see.

RICHARD. What have we got to eat, Mum?

RICHARD (*man*). Yes, what have we got to eat?

MOTHER (*drowsy*). Knobs of chairs and door handles . . .

RICHARD (*man*). Ah, go on — tell us.

MOTHER. 'me' dear, not 'us'. Wait and see pie.

RICHARD. Kippers and custard.

RICHARD (*man*). Sausage and mustard.

SUSAN. Semolina and frogspawn.

MOTHER. Hundreds of thousands. Barley-sugar sticks.

RICHARD (*man*). Sherbert fountains. Liquorice licks.

RICHARD. 'Here comes the fire brigade, all covered in marmalade.'

SUSAN. 'Yum yum, pig's bum, you can't have none.' (*Giggles.*)

MOTHER. Susan . . .

RICHARD (*man*). Picnics. Properly packed then. Sandwiches wrapped in greaseproof paper, crossed with elastic bands. Tomato, jam, fish-paste . . . Huge thermos flasks of dark, bitter tea with the milk in a separate little screwtop jar. Apples. Orange squash drunk from waxed paper Coronation cups. Sponge cake.

MOTHER. Chew it well dear. Eat it all up.

RICHARD (*man*). Think of the poor children in India.

MOTHER. They would be grateful for those crusts.

RICHARD. They hurt my teeth.

MOTHER. Build you up, make you strong.

RICHARD (*man*). Post-war austerity. Waste not, want not. Cabbage makes your hair curl.

SUSAN. That's silly.

MOTHER. What's silly, dear?

SUSAN. Cabbage can't make your hair curl.

MOTHER. Just a saying dear. Now help me lay the cloth.

RICHARD (*man*). Oh — I'd forgotten the cloth! Even on a picnic, miles from anywhere, among the meadowsweet and cornflowers, we spread a clean white linen tablecloth. Thus were the niceties preserved.

MOTHER. For what we are about to receive, may the Lord make us truly thankful.

SUSAN.
RICHARD. } Amen.

MOTHER. Now, a pack of sandwiches each. Open them up. Share them out. Richard, Susan.

SUSAN. I don't want a sandwich. I'm not hungry.

RICHARD. Can I have hers?

MOTHER. No you may not. Susan, I've gone to a lot of trouble over this picnic; you'll do me the courtesy of eating it.

SUSAN (*under her breath*). Sod your picnic.

Sound of a sharp slap.

SUSAN. Ow!

MOTHER. How dare you!!

SUSAN. You —

MOTHER. Don't you raise your hand to me, you filthy little slut!

SUSAN. That hurt.

MOTHER. It was meant to. Now apologise.

SUSAN. Let go of my hair!

MOTHER. Apologise!

SUSAN. Sorry . . .

MOTHER. You-are-never-to-use-language-like-that again do you hear? (*Beat.*) Do you?

SUSAN. Yes. (*She cries a little.*)

MOTHER. I don't know what's come over you these days. I really don't.

SUSAN. I just want to be treated like a grown-up.

MOTHER. When you behave like a grown-up, I'll treat you like one.

SUSAN. I knew you'd say that. You won't let me do any of the things my friends do.

MOTHER. Oh — such as?

SUSAN. Saturday morning pictures.

MOTHER. Cheap trash.

SUSAN. And Avril's allowed to wear lipstick.

MOTHER. Lipstick?! I'll not have any daughter of mine walking the streets like a painted harlot!

SUSAN. Painted harlot?!

MOTHER. It was that little guttersnipe Avril who taught you to swear, wasn't it?

RICHARD. What's a harlot?

MOTHER. Never mind.

SUSAN. It's a lady who charges money for . . .

MOTHER. Susan! I don't know, I've always tried to do the best for you . . .

SUSAN. Oh yes . . .

MOTHER. . . . and this is the thanks I get.

SUSAN. I don't see what's so wrong with lipstick. I bet Gran didn't stop you trying it.

MOTHER. *I* never wanted to look that common. And the only make-up I ever saw on your grandmother was what she called her little bit of fake.

SUSAN. What?

MOTHER. Her face powder.

SUSAN. Little bit of fake . . .

They laugh. An uneasy truce.

MOTHER. Dear Mother.

SUSAN. I wish she was still here; she'd know . . .

MOTHER. Yes. She would.

Pause.

RICHARD. Can I have some orange squash?

MOTHER. Please.

RICHARD. Please.

MOTHER. Days are always long enough to say please and thank you. Where are you going, Susan?

SUSAN. To stretch my legs.

MOTHER. I didn't hear you ask.

SUSAN. But we're in the middle of a field . . . !

MOTHER. Susan . . .

SUSAN. Oh — 'please may I get down?'

MOTHER. You may. Don't go near the railway line.

SUSAN. Don't worry, I shan't put *my* head on the track.

Pause.

RICHARD. Will the train be here soon?

MOTHER. No, not long now. You'll be able to see the smoke soon I expect.

RICHARD. D'you think the driver will blow his whistle when he sees us?

MOTHER. I don't think so. The railway company has strict regulations. He can't just blow the whistle anywhere.

RICHARD. But in the middle of the country.

MOTHER. I expect he'll wave.

RICHARD. Yes — but I'd like it if he blew the whistle.

Pause.

Mum — why did you and Susan fight?

MOTHER (*cautious*). Every family fights. It shows you love each other.

RICHARD (*baffled*). Oh, I see. (*Beat.*) Mum . . .

MOTHER. Yes?

RICHARD. Have I got to go on having piano lessons?

MOTHER. Yes.

RICHARD. But it's so hard. And boring.

MOTHER. Anything worth doing is hard work, dear. And your father would be so proud.

RICHARD. Could he play all that music at home?

MOTHER. Oh yes. Schumann, Brahms, Chopin. Chopin was his favourite.

RICHARD. Do you like that sort of music?

MOTHER. Yes, it's — very nice.

RICHARD (*man*). But you didn't understand it, did you?

MOTHER. I tried. And it pleased him if I listened.

RICHARD (*man*). So afterwards he played the popular tunes for you.

MOTHER. Every day, after dinner, before he went back to the office for the afternoon. 'There's a Song in my Heart.'

RICHARD (*man*). 'We'll Gather Lilacs.'

MOTHER. 'Marigold.' And now you can play like him. You're glad you learned, aren't you?

RICHARD (*man. Beat*). I'm glad.

RICHARD. Mum . . .

MOTHER. Mmm?

RICHARD. Can I go to boarding school?

MOTHER (*stunned out of her reverie*). What — did you say?

RICHARD. There's a boy at the Cubs whose brother goes and he says it's smashing.

MOTHER. But — why do you want to go away?

RICHARD. Well, I haven't got a dad have I and — well — I thought perhaps it would be better than being brought up by two women.

MOTHER (*laughing*). What nonsense!

RICHARD (*man*). Out of the mouths of babes and sucklings . . .

MOTHER. But — wouldn't you miss us, dear?

RICHARD. Oh yes — but I expect you get used to that.

MOTHER. Oh. Well, I don't know; I haven't thought. I — daresay it costs money. And I'm not a rich woman.

RICHARD. Didn't Dad leave you any money?

MOTHER (*beat*). No. Look, dear, why don't you go and join Susan while I clear away.

RICHARD. But promise you'll think about it?

MOTHER. I don't know.

RICHARD. Please.

MOTHER. All right, I promise. Now run along.

RICHARD. All right. (*Beat.*) I'd like to go, Mum. (*Calls.*) Susan can you see the smoke yet?

MOTHER. Not too near the edge. Well. My, my. What a day this is turning out to be.

RICHARD (*man*). Nothing at all for you to worry about.

MOTHER. A little boy who likes trains and a little girl making daisy-chains. Oh — I'm a poet and didn't know it. All perfectly normal . . .

RICHARD (*man*). But now she wants to wear lipstick and he wants to go to boarding school, of all things.

MOTHER. No . . .

RICHARD (*man*). And you're not strong enough to hold them.

MOTHER. I was too strong. (*Bitter.*) But still they went . . . (*Beat.*) 'Better than being brought up by two women' — who on earth put that poison into your head?

RICHARD (*man*). No-one. With all the uncluttered vision of an eight year old, I knew it.

MOTHER. So you went. Always what was best.

RICHARD (*man*). It wasn't easy for you.

MOTHER. No, it wasn't, my lad. Apart from the hurt, there was the expense . . . Not that I begrudged it.

RICHARD (*man*). No.

MOTHER. When — he died, I looked in my purse. I had two shillings and twopence. In the world. He never could *save.*

RICHARD (*man*). You did well.

MOTHER. Oh, I did well. You never wanted for anything. The Isle of Wight every summer.

RICHARD (*man*). Pocket-money every week.

MOTHER. Don't squander it now.

RICHARD (*man*). And — boarding school.

MOTHER. Yes. Did — did you enjoy it?

RICHARD (*man*). Every second.

MOTHER. So you didn't miss us?

RICHARD (*man*). Of course I did.

MOTHER (*relieved*). Ah. Well, I don't know, he's so young.

RICHARD (*man*). Let him go.

MOTHER. And Susan? Why doesn't she like me? I've tried to understand.

RICHARD (*man*). She'll come back.

MOTHER. Will she? Will they? So fragile, so innocent.

RICHARD (*man*). They'll survive.

MOTHER. But they're not ready. And neither am I.

RICHARD (*man. Anguish*). O Christ, let them *go*!

MOTHER (*brisk, back to normal*). We'll see, dear. Now that's everything cleared away. Clean and tidy, spick and span.

RICHARD. Mum, mum — come over here. See what Susan's made.

SUSAN. It's nothing special.

MOTHER. Coming. You see, they do need me. Now what have you been up to?

RICHARD. She's made a daisy chain.

MOTHER. Let me see. Susan, that's very clever.

RICHARD. How do you make them?

SUSAN. Make them, break them.

RICHARD. No, don't. Oh.

MOTHER. That wasn't necessary, dear. Such a pretty necklace.

SUSAN. I didn't mean to.

MOTHER. I know. Let's see how many different flowers we can find. Make a big bunch. Shall we?

SUSAN. All right.

MOTHER (*surprised*). You'd like to?

SUSAN. Yes, why not?

MOTHER. Well, then! Come on, Richard.

RICHARD. Can't I stay and wait for the train?

MOTHER. I promise we'll be back for the train.

RICHARD. Yes, but —

MOTHER. Now, off we go.

RICHARD (*man*). And off we went. Ambling ankle deep through the meadow; idling under trees; scrambling up banks. I lagged a little with anxious backward glances, looking for the smoke, only half hearing the litany of gentle names.

MOTHER. Rosebay willow herb, Ragged Robin, Lords and Ladies, Heartsease . . .

SUSAN. Where did you learn them all?

MOTHER. Nature Study, dear. When I was a girl.

RICHARD (*man*). And in the spring —

MOTHER. My favourite season. Bachelor's Buttons, Wood Anemones, Jack-by-the-Hedge, Celandine.

RICHARD. What's this one?

MOTHER. Sorrel. We used to eat that.

RICHARD. Ugh!

SUSAN. Is that true?

MOTHER. I'm not in the habit of making things up dear . . . No! And young hawthorn leaves. We called them Bread and Cheese.

SUSAN. Bread and cheese.

MOTHER. Say please.

RICHARD. Dock leaves. Stops the stinging.

MOTHER. Bindweed.

SUSAN. Dog rose.

RICHARD. Dead-nettle.

MOTHER. King cup.

SUSAN. Buttercup.

RICHARD. Honeysuckle.

RICHARD (*man*). A wild garden, wide as the sky.

MOTHER. He liked to garden.

RICHARD (*man*). Grew gardenias . . .

MOTHER. . . . for his button-hole.

RICHARD. Stocks.

SUSAN. Phlox.

RICHARD. Hollyhocks.

RICHARD (*man*). Love lies bleeding.

MOTHER (*beat*). Love lies bleeding . . .

RICHARD (*man*). And back we came with a big, blowsy bunch, blue and green, red and yellow. Later, it would be carried all the way home . . .

SUSAN. Mummy, my arms ache.

MOTHER. Not far to go.

SUSAN. Let me leave them in the hedge.

MOTHER. So sad, abandoned flowers.

RICHARD (*man*). — and revived at last in the large white china jug in the kitchen. There they remained, finally forgotten, dead and dusty.

MOTHER. There, what a fine collection.

SUSAN. I'm hot.

MOTHER. Who'd like some orange squash?

RICHARD. Cor — is there some left?

SUSAN. I thought we drank it all.

MOTHER (*triumphant*). I kept some back. My surprise.

RICHARD (*man*). Always some kept back. Another sweet in the bag. Another penny in the purse. And still the sun burned in the sky. Cows flicked their tails under the trees. And then very quietly, I remember, Susan spoke.

SUSAN. I can see the smoke.

RICHARD. Where? Where's the smoke? Can you really see it? Mum . . .

RICHARD (*man*). A terrible excitement in my eyes, an unknown fear, in my stomach.

RICHARD (*near hysteria*). The train's coming! The train . . . look at the smoke!

MOTHER (*firmly*). Richard, calm down.

SUSAN. Stupid train.

RICHARD. Oh come on, hurry, hurry. We'll miss it, we'll *miss* it!

MOTHER. Richard! You know very well there is plenty of time.

RICHARD. There isn't, there isn't!

MOTHER. Look — the signal hasn't even changed yet.

RICHARD. Oh, please . . .

RICHARD (*man*). Of course! Each detail gradually being filled in. A hundred yards along the line, tucked in at the end of the cutting, stood the signal, operated by a series of levers and pulleys at the bidding of some distant railway company hand. And in the middle of that summer quiet would come a clunk, and be enacted a weird semaphore that made the rooks rise, circle and settle again.

RICHARD (*calling*). I can see the signal from here. Oh come *on* you two.

MOTHER. We'd better go. There'll be no peace until we do.

SUSAN. Oh, all right.

MOTHER. Susan, what's the matter? D'you really not like trains?

SUSAN. What is there to like?

MOTHER. But you enjoy our trips to the sea-side, don't you?

SUSAN. I like the seaside, but not the train. The smell, the noise. I don't like those men in uniform, laughing and winking at me, with their big blue cases blocking the corridor. And the seats are so prickly: and those brown and white photographs of seaside towns — it's all so depressing. And I don't like getting smuts in my eyes . . .

MOTHER. You shouldn't lean out of the window. There is a notice.

SUSAN. Oh, Mum, don't you understand! You have to lean out of windows sometimes, even if it's only once in your whole life. But worse than all of that, I know that whatever I do, one day I'll have to work in an office and everyday, twice a day, I'll ride in a train. I'll sit opposite big-bellied men with shiny shoes and folded newspapers. And no-one will ever speak to me. Travel down the years in silence. (*Bitter.*) And *that's* why I don't like trains.

MOTHER. You work hard at school dear, you'll get a good job.

SUSAN. Oh, what's the point?

MOTHER. The point is, you'll get used to the train.

RICHARD. Mum, Susan, look! You can really see the smoke now!

MOTHER. So you can. It'll soon be here.

RICHARD. Listen! Listen . . . I can *hear* it.

Sound of a distant 0-6-0 tank engine. To be held under and modulated as specified in the script.

RICHARD (*man*). And faintly, across the stillness came the first steady rhythm. No going back now. I was caught.

RICHARD. Oh just listen . . . When we get home I'm going to get my train set out. I'll lay it out in the garden and wind it up and watch it go round and round . . .

RICHARD (*man*). And invent a time-table and imagine passengers in the painted tin carriages . . .

RICHARD. And load the trucks with coal and cars, chickens, timber . . .

RICHARD (*man*). And our curious cat will sit in the middle, nerves a-twitch, and watch the tin train run round and round . . .

RICHARD. I'll stay until it's dark.

MOTHER. Time for bed.

RICHARD. Oh . . .

MOTHER. Lord keep us safe this night.

RICHARD. Can I have a drink of water?

MOTHER. Go to sleep . . .

RICHARD (*man*). And in the dark I would lie listening to the engine working in the goods yard a mile away. The sound of trucks being shunted would eventually lull me to sleep.

RICHARD (*drowsy*). Over the points, over the points, over the points, over the . . .

RICHARD (*man*). And in dreams I regularly saw a huge black hissing engine towering over me, and standing on the footplate, smiling, was a little girl in a white frock.

RICHARD *moans slightly, as a child in a nightmare, under the rest of the speech.*

And I would wake, a terrible excitement in my eyes, a fear in my stomach, calling . . .

RICHARD. Mum, mum.

MOTHER. Hush dear. Only a dream.

RICHARD. Mum, mum, look. The smoke's coming nearer. Almost round the curve. Listen.

Sound of a train in the middle distance.

MOTHER. When I was married . . .

SUSAN (*beat*). Mummy?

MOTHER (*reverie*). When I was married the month was June. Nineteen-thirty-seven. The King crowned a few weeks before. A day like today. The town turned out, it seemed. The newspaper came, a photograph on the front page, and a report: 'Well known and popular young teacher'. I took my father's arm and held on tight. He'd bought a new pair of gloves. Mother cried. Your father wore his gardenia. We had our reception at the Imperial Hotel (of course, it was *somewhere*, in those days, not like now). It must have cost Dad the earth. Afterwards we walked down the steps to Mr Sargent's best car, all shining black and beribboned and he drove us across the square to the railway station. All of forty yards. How everyone laughed. And the station-master, Mr Livingstone, came out and shook your father's hand and kissed me on the cheek. And we all laughed again. Then the guard wished us luck — I taught his little boy, you know; what *was* his name? — and we climbed into the carriage. Mr Livingstone ran up to the engine and whispered something to the driver and they both looked mighty pleased with themselves. The flag waved, the whistle blew, and we pulled away. We leaned out of the window — yes, just once in my life I leaned out — and waved and waved. Then, just as we reached the end of the platform, there were two deafening bangs. My heart beat so! (*A little laugh.*) They'd let off two fog detonators, like a gun salute! We looked back down the platform and saw Mr Livingstone laughing, fit to bust. Next day we caught the Cornish Express from Paddington. It was all such fun. When I was married.

RICHARD (*man*). Now another Coronation, another train. And will he be coming back on this one?

MOTHER. Don't, please.

Sound of the train.

RICHARD (*man*). Then suddenly, in the still of the afternoon, the sound of the approaching engine grew louder. It was nearly out of the curve. We all held our breath and I strained on tip-toe.

RICHARD. The signal! Watch the signal!

RICHARD (*man*). Any moment now.

RICHARD. Come on, come *on*!

Beat. Sound effects.

RICHARD (*man*). And at last down swung the signal.

Sound effects and all three cheer.

The rooks rose, and with a flurry of noise, the train appeared at the end of the cutting, hissing and puffing, moving steadily on its crazy journey from nowhere to nowhere.

RICHARD. There it is! There it is!

Sound effects loud now.

MOTHER. What a lot of smoke! Come on Susan.

RICHARD (*man*). Louder and louder.

RICHARD. Nearer and nearer.

MOTHER. Get ready to wave, my dears.

RICHARD. Look! I can see the driver! Please, please, wave . . .

RICHARD (*man*). Along the cutting, over the tracks, huffing and puffing, into the open, into the sunshine, filling our lives. And-we-Waved!

RICHARD. }
SUSAN.   }   Hurray!

SUSAN. Can they see us, can they? The smoke . . .

RICHARD. The driver's waving. Look, he's waving! Hullo, hullo!

MOTHER. }
SUSAN. }   Hullo!

RICHARD (*man*). Now it's almost level. Will he, won't he, will he, won't he . . . ?

Sound of train whistle.

RICHARD (*ecstatic*). Y-e-s!!! He blew the whistle!

RICHARD (*man*). Joy of joys! The noise tremendous, the sight fantastic, the smell intoxicating. I thought my heart would burst.

RICHARD. He blew the whistle . . .

MOTHER. Wave my darlings, wave! Oh God.

RICHARD (*man*). Behind the engine, two red and cream carriages swinging along. Curious faces looking up, smiling gently, waving shyly.

MOTHER. }
RICHARD. }   Hullo, hullo.

SUSAN. There's the guard.

RICHARD. Hullo, guard!

RICHARD (*man*). As the train passed, the guard, a ruddy faced smiling man, with a ginger moustache, waved magnificently.

RICHARD. Hullo . . .

RICHARD (*man*). And as suddenly as it had appeared the little procession was now receding, steam billowing from every crack, every joint.

MOTHER. Goodbye . . . !

SUSAN. Goodbye.

RICHARD. Goodb-y-e!

Sound of the whistle, slightly distant, receding.

ALL. Hurray!

RICHARD. He did it again!

RICHARD (*man*). And I climbed the fence and waved until my arm ached; until the diminishing carriages vanished around the distant bend.

MOTHER. There now (*A sigh of exhaustion.*) wasn't that *fun*!

SUSAN. If only they were all like that . . .

RICHARD. It's gone. Smashing . . .

RICHARD (*man*). And we sat for a moment or two, silent in our own worlds, getting our breath back. Then, inevitably . . .

MOTHER. Time to go home.

RICHARD. Oh . . .

MOTHER. Susan, you carry the flowers. Richard, you fold up the groundsheet.

RICHARD. Wasn't it smashing when he blew the whistle?

MOTHER. And how the guard waved.

RICHARD. Can we come again?

MOTHER. We'll see, dear.

SUSAN. And one day, just once, can I go down the town and . . .

MOTHER. — sit in a café with your friends? (*She laughs.*) We'll have to see about that too. Careful with the flowers now. Richard come along.

RICHARD (*beat*). I don't want to go back.

MOTHER (*gently*). No . . . But there are no more trains today. So — off we go.

RICHARD (*man*). The sun was lower in the sky now, a deeper gold, as we walked back across the meadow. Our conversation grew sporadic and finally ceased. Each given up to a private world:

SUSAN. 'Whatever I do, one day I'll have to work in an office and no-one will ever speak to me . . . '

RICHARD. 'Perhaps I'll have to catch a train when I go to boarding school . . . '

MOTHER. 'How everyone laughed! It was all such fun. When I was married.'

RICHARD (*man*). No — I don't want to go back either. There's a housing estate in that field now; the railway line was taken up years ago. But the past is always with us. And lately I've begun to remember those long summer afternoons. So that when I'm in a train now, I find myself occasionally looking up and gazing through the window at the June countryside speeding by. Because I know that under the next bridge, across the next field, on top of the next embankment, I'll suddenly see them again. There they'll be: a woman in a print frock, her hands resting gently on the shoulders of a little girl and boy. A strange little trio, all in sunhats and sandals, standing in a line. Smiling. And they'll be waving to a train.

MARTYR OF THE HIVES

by Peter Redgrove

Peter Redgrove was born in 1932. He read Natural Sciences at Cambridge, has worked as a research scientist, scientific editor and journalist, was visiting poet to Buffalo University, U.S.A., Gregory Fellow in poetry at Leeds University, visiting professor at Colgate University, U.S.A., and now works in a West Country art school. He has published nine books of poetry, the latest of which, *The Weddings at Nether Powers*, was a Poetry Book Society Choice in 1979. In 1978 his radio play *The God of Glass* won the Imperial Tobacco Award for an Original Single Play, and the following year he published a novel of the same name based on the play. His latest novel, *The Beekeepers*, is his sixth. His first, *In the Country of the Skin*, won the Guardian Fiction Prize for 1973. A non-fiction study of the human fertility cycle, *The Wise Wound*, written with Penelope Shuttle, was published by Penguin in 1980.

Martyr of the Hives was first broadcast on BBC Radio 4 on 15th October 1980. The cast was as follows:

HENRY	Richard Morant
HANGER	John Franklyn-Robbins
JULIA	Hildegard Neil
PAUL	John Justin
BEEKEEPER	Martin Friend
JAMES	Leonard Fenton
LIBRARIAN	Rex Holdsworth
JENNIE	Catherine Owen

Director: Brian Miller

Bee-noise in this scene, varying with action.

BEEKEEPER. Let me help you with your veil.

HENRY. It's OK. Just these stray long bits.

BEEKEEPER. Nevertheless. It's quite important. They could be fierce little beggars.

HENRY. I love that description of the OM of the Indian saint: the humming he does in meditation. 'Like the sound of love-crazed bees'.

BEEKEEPER. Now the gloves. There! Now we can look into the hives. The tops are simply like lids of packing-cases. You lift them off. Then you see the racks of wax honeycomb full of bees.

HENRY. Won't you wear gloves?

BEEKEEPER. I've been a beekeeper fifty years. I was a beekeeper before I was a schoolmaster. Oh they won't sting me. I'm almost a member of the hives. My skin very likely smells like bees to them. You're a different matter, especially if you've never visited hives before.

HENRY. Yes. I swell up.

BEEKEEPER. Well be careful! It's dangerous if you get stung in the eye-ball. I lift the top, so. Now the little pacifier, the 'puffer'. You saw me light the burning paper. I puff the smoke round and that makes them sleepy. I remove any combs. You can lift the combs out, see.

HENRY. What a sight! There are so many. All glistening, like a dark liquid that sings. Thousands and thousands, hanging like black grapes. They're safe, quite safe?

BEEKEEPER. Little can get through the veil, or the gloves.

HENRY. Each bee is so exact, like some jewel. Amber and gold and jet. Each one singing with its wings, which glitter like water. How many are there here, in this hive?

BEEKEEPER. About twenty thousand. Their food is flowers now, but they were once meat-eaters. If they'd not evolved and become vegetarians, we'd not be talking now. Bees pollinate the flowers, and this is how flowers evolved into the trees of the forest where man evolved.

HENRY. Then it is as the yogis say, this hum. It is the sound of life-energy, time, evolution.

BEEKEEPER. I prefer to think of it as the sound of satisfaction. OM if you like, but I like to say AH-HM like a satisfying stretch.

HENRY. You're teasing me a bit, I know. You're used to the bees, but I've never seen them before. They're very impressive. Each of these wooden boxes on stilts humming like a powerhouse.

BEEKEEPER. Since I retired from teaching boys Latin, I have studied the ways of bees, not men. Bees live in harmony, for their public good, and ours. You are listening to the sound of that harmony. *Fit sonitus mussantque oras et limina circum.*

HENRY. That will be Virgil's bees, I expect!

BEEKEEPER. Who else? 'What a murmuring you hear as they drone around their policies and doorsteps!' You talk of power! You should see thirsty bees swarming. And yet they can be gentle to those they know. I once knew an American beemaster who could make them swarm into a beard around his lips, and he was once photographed taking a shower in this beard of bees.

HENRY. He would hum to them, and they'd cling humming to his lips.

BEEKEEPER. It's quite true. I'll show you the cutting. He was an ordinary beekeeper like me. Then there was that other man, who could do strange things with the bees, and made a religion of it.

HENRY. A religion?

BEEKEEPER. He was called Practique. It was quite a large movement in its day. There was some mystery about his disappearance. Of course his disciples said that he'd been caught up on a gigantic beeswing to heaven!

HENRY. A religion!

BEEKEEPER. Oh, it's quite easy to make a religion of it, if you're so minded. I'm even a little bit religious about them myself. But that's just mutual kindness between us. I wouldn't dream of saying the things that Practique taught, even though I do happen to think they're true, in some senses.

HENRY. What teachings!

BEEKEPHERS. Practique taught that there is a harmony everywhere in the air and the earth, and that the bees make this harmony plain to all the senses. You can hear it in the hum. You can see it in their strictly-built cities of hexagonal wax. You can taste it in their honey and comb. It was said that he would teach his initiates to touch and feel it too, by plunging their arms into the hives and letting the bees crawl over the naked skins of their entire bodies. If you flinched, you were unfit. If they stung you you were not suited to become a high disciple. If you endured their multifarious touch then, it is said, it gave you transports of ecstacy.

HENRY. I'd be no good. I'm ticklish.

BEEKEEPER. Oh, it was quite serious. The man who's got my job now was an initiate of Practique!

HENRY. What, here? In the village?

BEEKEEPER. Mr Hanger. It helped him get the job. Oh, not because of the religion. He offered to teach the boys some of the exercises in his spare time.

HENRY. What exercises?

BEEKEEPER. I don't know. You can go along there if you like. It's in the Scout-hut, at the edge of the stream at the other side of the Green. His coming here put me in mind of all this, but it was all a bit much for me, despite my devotion to bees. Maybe because of it. I love the sweetness and light of the bees. I polish my tables with beeswax and I light my dinner-table with beeswax candles. The bees make their wax from the plants, and the plants drink up the sunshine. The candles store the sunlight and give it back to me in my house at night. And like the flowers my body feeds on the sunshine in the honey they make. All perfectly natural, the circling of energy in the world. Yet so — wonderful.

HENRY. And Practique's teachings?

BEEKEEPER. Went too far! It was a mystery, but it was also an industry. Of course bees are the mirror of nature. So are we! He taught that people can evolve by watching this rustling, humming mirror of the hives, to see mankind's future in the glittering of wings. Practique's people would spend long hours staring into the hives, seeing pictures, meditating. They would perch on tall stools looking into the open hives like open books, humming. They would saturate their bodies with bee-products: the women would dress their hair with honey and wax; all would go on diets of pollen, propolis, royal jelly. It was said they buried their dead like pupae in honey, ready for the great winged resurrection that would on the Day of Judgment pour and swarm out of the great humming top and hive of the earth.

HENRY. And God a great bee, hovering above them . . .

BEEKEEPER. Of course. But a queen-bee. A Goddess. And all the bee-blessed would hang shining in the sky like the stars twinkling, eating honeycomb for ever, and the beating of their wings would blow this wicked earth away!

HENRY. But the Master vanished . . .

BEEKEEPER. And the pupils eventually drifted away. Yet you still meet one now and again. Like our Mr Hanger down the lane. Look — you've been stung!

HENRY. Have I? It didn't hurt.

BEEKEEPER. Let me brush it away. Poor bee. That little pasty mass on your forearm is the guts of it, attached still to the sting, which is barbed and buried in your flesh.

HENRY. There's no swelling. I thought it would have injected me with its agony. I feel more alive! But that's all the new things you've told me. Thank you very much. Can I go and see this Mr Hanger?

BEEKEEPER. If you want to. Say I sent you. He wants to borrow my hives. For meditation. Let me help you off with your gauntlets, and your veil.

Bee sound out.

Pause.

HANGER. There is a chair for you Mr Esmond. Just outside the exercise area.

HENRY. What a lot of boys.

HANGER. Yes, it's a good attendance.

HENRY. The uniforms symbolise — bees, I suppose. I can see that in the little close-fitting skull-caps, and the short dusky yellow and brown jackets with the banded sleeves to signify several joints — more than one elbow in fact — but what are the big yellow patch-pockets on the trousers.

HANGER. They stand for the pollen-sacs.

HENRY. This is very elaborate for village boys whose parents I expect haven't much cash.

HANGER. Mothers will always find a way if its a question of uniforms.

HENRY. There's one thing missing though.

HANGER. What is that?

HENRY. Why, Mr Hanger, the wings.

HANGER. The wings are invisible when the bee is flying, Mr Esmond.

HENRY. These boys are not flying.

HANGER. Flying, in a sense, is the purpose of the exercises I teach.

HENRY. These are Practique's exercises.

HANGER. Indeed they are. You have been gossiping with the old schoolmaster.

HENRY. Please believe me, I am very interested. May I see your sword.

HANGER. It is a sharpened rush that has been painted with a gold hilt and amber blade. We call it a 'sting'. It is purely symbolic.

HENRY. Only some of the older boys are wearing them.

HANGER. You have to earn your sting.

HENRY. But surely it is the drone which is the virile male, and drones have no stings.

HANGER. It is the workers which have the stings, and the workers are maiden bees. They cannot be anything else. They have no reproductive apparatus. They are a kind of eternal spinster. Sexless, as the angels are said to be.

HENRY. Or like the castrated choirboys of the mediaeval church.

HANGER. Now what are you getting at, Mr Esmond. I assure you you would find any of my fully-trained boys most formidable.

HENRY. I am only trying to learn, Mr Hanger.

HANGER. Then let me tell you a thing or two. Or, better, show you. *Now bees . . .*

HENRY. Not boys, but bees . . .

HANGER. *Now bees, let me hear your wings.*

Humming, mounting in intensity.

This is a breathing-exercise, Mr Esmond. Apis mellifica, the honey-bee, vibrates its wings 200 times a second, that is, 12,000 times a minute. That is the hum. Human boys cannot use their muscles or their limbs in any such fashion as the honey-bee does. But there is one way they can make such vibrations. They can do it with their little windpipes and lungs, and the resonating cavities or sinuses in their chests and foreheads. These are used like the pipes and resonators in a church organ. The hum, properly taught and practised, is very beneficial to their physiology and development. The breaths are even and deep. The air, with its enriching oxygen, is retained for a correct period of time. The vibration massages all the internal organs. The boys get what you could call 'high' perfectly naturally without recourse to drugs, alcohol, tobacco or girls. This is how they 'fly'. It is the natural vigour coursing round the body like electricity, and like the small powerhouse it is, giving off its energetic sound, as Practique taught, the ground note of the universe, the sound of bees. Listen, and allow the note and patterns of its resonance to form images within you, and you will learn meditation as Practique taught it. As he used to say: 'By means of the bees, we concentrate the ecstatic forces within us, and these resemble the bees themselves. By doing this, wonderful images form in the honeycomb of the brain.'

HENRY. But where is Practique now?

HANGER. Our belief is that he is now out of time. Like the busy sun and the busy bee, he has condensed his energy into stillness. It is stillness like the stillness of the tall candle of wax. He is in eternity. He is eternity.

HENRY. These boys are not still, they rustle and vibrate.

HANGER. None of us here is perfect, yet.

HENRY. When one is, will he disappear, like Practique, and the police have to be called?

HANGER. Please don't trifle with us, Mr Esmond. You may suffer from it. Our body here, our corporate body, may be vibrating 200 times a second, but our mind is still, held in that hum. This is con-centr-ation, holding to a centre.

(*To the class*:) No, no, bees, that is not good. You will not earn your stings that way. I will turn on the tape-recording. You must take your pitch from that, the alert but contented hive, ready to expel predators.

HENRY. So you use this tape-recorder to train them?

HANGER. These are the sounds of Practique's own hives. You will hear the recordings change with the emotions of the hives under attack, in sunshine, in cold weather.

(*To the class*:) Now the angry wounded hive. Follow it, bees! Assume the fighting stance.

HENRY. All the little black bees-knees bent in their tight trousers and the little gloved knuckles gleaming! Why, Mr Hanger, these are martial arts.

HANGER. Only when necessary. When there is an intruder, Mr Esmond. When there is an enemy to the hive. Are you an enemy of our hive?

HENRY. You said that they were meditating. But the boys are marching forward in ranks, hitting at the empty air!

HANGER. And if any of those blows landed, Mr Esmond, they would break bone, they would sting!

HENRY. But you said it was a meditation-class.

HANGER. Each boy strikes his opponent with perfect stillness in his heart, and without anger.

HENRY. I don't suppose that's much comfort to the opponent.

HANGER. Those who break the sanctity of the hive deserve suffering.

HENRY. The hive? What is the hive?

HANGER. It is not built yet. It is here. (*He stamps his feet.*) On this ground. It is England, as she will be, mighty yet. These are native English bees, and woe betide the foreigner when they are grown into their strength. I shall show you how our youngest bee-boy here can smash a granite block with his little sting.

HENRY. With his *what*?

HANGER. His fist, Mr Esmond, the clenched clean-living hand of a little British bee. I shall show you how they learn to survey the terrain and report the position of an invader at headquarters by means of their waggle-dance and their round-dance, and how they find their way unaided across country like skilful soldier-bees by the position of the sun, reporting back by dance. And I shall show you how they adore the Queen.

HENRY. They are almost running, and their fists striking blows faster and faster. Hanger, do you have control of these boys?

HANGER. You had better hum like me, Mr Esmond, and do as I do.

(*To the class*:) Now, bees, the loyal salutation. Bees, the Queen.

BOYS.
HANGER. } THE QUEEN, GOD BLESS HER MAJESTY.

HANGER. Mr Esmond?

HENRY (*hastily*). God Bless Her Majesty indeed.

HANGER. That fragrant breath from healthy lungs cools the hive, does it not, Mr Esmond. Do you not feel the zest in the air, like the smell of bees? You do not understand our bee-ing, Mr Esmond. The Bees are restless. They are not sure of you yet. You must pass our test.

(*To the class*:) Bees, is he one of us? Is he an intruder who will contaminate us? Bees, smell out this intruder with your feelers!

HENRY. Your boys. What are they doing? They are breaking ranks. I'm as English as you are, boys. Are they going to beat me, Hanger? No, boys, don't . . . they're touching me all over . . . don't, boys, I'm ticklish . . . get off, get off . . .

Uncontrollable giggling and laughter from HENRY, *buzzing and laughter from the boys, mocking laughter from* HANGER. HENRY *breaks away. The sound of running footsteps across planking, the slamming of a door. The relative silence of open air with* HENRY *panting, outside, escaped.*

HENRY. Mad. All mad as . . . all crazy . . . as Bees in Spring.

Pause.

Bully boys. Bully bees. Was this what Practique taught? A city-state crammed with boys in bee-clothes. Proto-fascist bee-marches. Salutes with the closed fist?

HENRY (*to the* LIBRARIAN). Excuse me.

LIBRARIAN. Yes?

HENRY. I'd like to see the newspaper files for 1970, please.

LIBRARIAN. English?

HENRY. Of course I'm English. What do you mean?

LIBRARIAN. I want to know whether it's the English papers you want for 1970. Or is it the Spanish, the French, the American? They're all here.

HENRY. Like a great wasp-nest of paper.

LIBRARIAN. No, Sir. We have them all on microfilm nowadays.

HENRY. I'd like to see the *Guardian* files, the *Mail*, the *Times*, and the two Sundays.

LIBRARIAN. Which two Sundays?

HENRY. The *Observer* and the *News of the World*, of course. Oh yes, and I'd like to see the local paper too.

LIBRARIAN. What area?

HENRY. London . . . but what part . . . I don't know exactly where it happened . . .

LIBRARIAN. Perhaps I can help. What happening are you attempting to trace?

HENRY. The Practique Disappearance. The Bee-Prophet who disappeared.

LIBRARIAN. That was at Stainton Square, Sir. You want the Kensington files.

HENRY. That's astonishingly helpful. Did you just remember . . . or were you perhaps involved in some way?

LIBRARIAN. I keep bees in my spare time. I was interested in Practique's claims. When I heard that his religion involved bathing in them, I turned off. No wonder he disappeared. Eaten by his bees, I shouldn't wonder.

HENRY. Bees are vegetarian.

LIBRARIAN. I expect he just decamped with the cash-box. I like bees, but not in that way. They help me think orderly. I redesigned the filing system in this library on the model of the honeycomb. So if you will come this way, I'll put the reels on the microfilm viewer for you. You notice these sound-proofed hexagonal reading-spaces? Efficient and decorative, I think.

HENRY. If a bee walked up to your desk and asked for the Kensington newspaper files, I expect he'd feel quite at home here.

LIBRARIAN. Oh we try to please as many requirements as possible, Sir.

Fade out and in to HENRY *reading.*

Bee-noise in the background.

HENRY. Here it is. 'Amazing Disappearance of Bee-Prophet'. 'Police were baffled last night when they were called to the headquarters of the famous Bee-Cult in Kensington's Stainton Square. Disciples of self-styled Beemaster Adrian Practique milled around in confusion like bees who had lost their queen. As titled debutante Hon Julia Messenger explained: "He simply did not come. That is all I can say." The Honourable Julia was stunningly attired in velvet skullcap and tight amber-and-gold trousers with yellow patch pockets, the religious uniform of a senior member of the Order. Paul Masterson, right hand man of Prophet Practique told the police that the Master simply had not arrived at the rally. He was billed to appear as cantor in a work especially commissioned from the famous West German composer Heinz Minnit. This was 'Hymn of the Bees' and was described as avant-guarde community-singing. According to other disciples Practique had arrived in his chauffeur-driven limousine and had entered the building. Apparently he did not arrive in the Hall where his co-religionists expectantly awaited him. The police do not suspect foul play, but Scotland Yard's Fraud Squad are currently investigating the cult's accounts. It is also rumoured that the Inland Revenue are to call for an audit.' It looks as if he did do a bunk, then. I wonder what the Fraud Squad found. They'd probably keep it to themselves. Here's a good picture of Practique! Colour supplement . . . opulent pictures of bees, and crowds of devoted worshippers all in their skull-caps, humming as though they had wings. Practique looks good. A fit sixty, I'd say. I can't say he looks phoney. He's one of those fortunates who don't go grey. Dark beard, tanned skin — sunlamps probably, though he has a temple — correction: 'hive' — in sunny California. Wears a cloak with his bee-outfit, made to look like veined folded wings. Nice ceremonial sword — correction: 'sting' — at his hip. Real gold and amber by the look of it. Reflective, slightly mocking *Observer* article about the cult. No mention of fraud or Inland Revenue prosecution. That seemed to fizzle out as an explanation. Just one big question, a big blank — where did Practique go, how did he disappear? There seems to be no answer beyond the religious one. I wonder . . . Strange things were said about this cult, according to the articles: 'The ancient world esteemed the bees as spiritual beings, something between the plant-world and the animals. They were mediators, the messengers of the spirits. Unlike the terrible blood-sacrifices of the animal-worshippers, the honey was sacrificed to the earth-goddesses. The bee symbolised the never-resting work of the earth-spirit, its artful business. Their humming was the sound made by the resurrecting dead when they sported in the Elysian Fields . . . ' I'm sure there's more to this than meets the eye. It's not just fascistical bullying, martial arts, avantgarde and health food sales. There's something more. And at the heart of it is Practique's disappearance. A wise and beautiful religion like this couldn't just fail. I must go where it all finished. Number Six, Stainton Square.

Fade out bee-noise.

Fade in to sounds of tearing and splintering wood, footsteps on uncarpeted floor, echoes of an empty house.

Hallo! Is anybody at home?

Echoes passing away. At the edge of the echoes, the dive-bombing sound of a bee or wasp.

Get off! There's something caught in here with me. Hornets? Sounds like a bee or wasp. Get away!

He strikes out. The bee-noise changes to elusive silvery laughter echoing, dying away, tantalising.

Who's that? A shadow darting down the stairs! I know you're there. I can see you! No I can't.

Splintering and tearing sounds as he rips boards off the windows.

Let's get some light in here. Now I can see you. What are you doing here. Who are you?

JULIA. I might ask you the same.

HENRY. Just a minute. There's a bee or wasp caught in here.

JULIA. I loved to do that in church when I was a little girl. Those stuffy Sundays in the family pew. I wanted to upset God. Listen. (*She does the dive-bombing impression again.*) The place where I sat against the hollow pillar made an echo-chamber, a whispering gallery. I'd make the dive-bombing sounds and everybody would duck. (*Dive-bombing impression.*) It was best during the sermon. Once a bee gets into the church how do you get it out? The vicar in his pulpit would swipe out at it, just when he was blessing us. People began to see it everywhere. I made them see it everywhere. (*Dive-bombing impression.*) A bee in church is a fearsome thing. It could be a wasp. Could be a hornet. It could be that burr on a hat, that spot of candle-wax on a pew. People would slap at each other with the fat hymn-books. Who are you, please?

HENRY. I do beg your pardon. I fear I am trespassing. I knew the story of this place. I couldn't resist the loose board on the door. Please excuse me. I'll leave immediately.

JULIA. No! Don't go yet. The story of this place. What could you know about that. Come closer so I can see you. Are you a reporter?

HENRY. I'm afraid not. Are you a squatter?

JULIA. I own the house.

HENRY. Practique's house.

JULIA. You knew Him.

HENRY. Not I. But I want to learn all I can about him.

JULIA. I loved him. I loved this house where he gave us so much. And he gave it to me before he — went.

HENRY. I know this is where it happened.

JULIA. What happened? What exactly do you think happened?

HENRY. I didn't mean to upset you.

JULIA. What happened?

HENRY. Well, the disappearance. The non-arrival, like you said in the paper. Nothing happened.

JULIA. That's all right then.

HENRY. I just wanted to find out more.

JULIA. Why, there's nothing more. You're rather nice. You're not a policeman?

HENRY. No! Certainly not. What have the police to do with this now? It seemed to me such a strange and compelling religion, with somewhere wisdom and beauty in it. I want to know why it disappeared, why it failed.

JULIA. It did not fail!

HENRY. I beg your pardon, again. But you must admit that the Master of it disappeared without warning. I've met a man who turns little boys into bullies with the aid of Practique exercises, and I saw a library that was organised like a honeycomb, and the headquarters are derelict, with you like a kind of ghost haunting them . . .

JULIA. I'm not a ghost. Touch me.

HENRY. Ah, well, no you're not a ghost.

JULIA. It's not derelict upstairs. I'll show you.

HENRY. But what happened at the end? It was a great occasion. All the initiates were there. Instead — a disappearance.

JULIA. Something was shown. It altered us all.

HENRY. But the Master didn't arrive.

JULIA. Oh yes he did. As never before.

HENRY. Nobody saw him leave.

JULIA. He came into our meeting and left with us. I took an oath not to tell. We all did.

HENRY. I'll take an oath.

JULIA. I've already said more than I should.

HENRY. You haven't really told me anything.

JULIA. You can't take an oath down here. Come upstairs where I can see you better.

Fade out.

Fade in to creaking stairs and the low crying of a baby.

HENRY. You do live here then. What an interesting cradle. Like a hexagonal brood-chamber of a bee. It even looks like wax.

JULIA. Heavy-duty polythene. They were mass-produced for his children. We were all given one when we were initiated as queens.

HENRY. All of you? Is this Practique's child?

JULIA. There were thirteen queens. Now there are only Jenny and Anne and me. Let me introduce you. (*Sounds of women's garments swishing and faint giggling.*) We all help each other now. No, it's not His child, alas. He left no children after all. Jenny, Anne, look who I've found. It's . . . what's your name?

HENRY. Henry.

JULIA. We'll call you Harry. Harry, I think you know too much and too little. You said you'd take an oath. You must be initiated first. As queens we are empowered to give you entry. We will show you the secret heart of our religion, almost the last secret. Ladies, will you make yourselves ready? Harry, come with me.

Footsteps. Pause. The whine of machinery.

HENRY. Great heavy red curtains cover the wall, drawing without a speck of dust, yet downstairs looks as though it had been abandoned for a century! There are doors here. They look as though they are made of gold!

JULIA. It is the wealth of our church. See what is behind them.

HENRY. They are poised on their hinges, glide open like wings almost without sound, only whispers . . . and there, behind . . . a great gold altar covered with an amber cloth, twining pillars carved with gold open-winged queen bees in flight!

JULIA. It is a bed, Harry.

HENRY. The doors are closing.

JULIA. You wanted to know our religion. There is an exercise you would not learn from Mr Hanger. Yes — we knew Hanger. Perhaps if the Master had not — disappeared — Hanger and his kind would have taken over. It was the manner of his going that defeated Hanger's plans.

HENRY. You promised to tell me.

JULIA. I have not yet administered the oath. I said the child outside was not Practique's. Yet he planned a new kind of man, a second generation of Practiques that would be taught about bees from their earliest years, fed from babyhood on pollen, royal jelly, honey. I have seen Practique clothed in a living robe of bees. I have seen his skin darken with the fertility of them, a glittering man of bees, with a humming skin that spoke words and which crawled in patterns like living tattoos.

HENRY. The bees spoke!

JULIA. I will show you soon. We wanted this man's child.

HENRY. What a man he must have been.

JULIA. He was sterile, Harry. He was not a drone, after all. We could not go together on our wedding-flight.

HENRY. But that was the whole purpose . . .

JULIA. Oh, we could make love! But there were no sperms. His semen was analysed. It was sweet-tasting, like a honey, and clear as crystal, but with no sperms at all.

HENRY. And you say his body spoke.

Bee hum: JULIA *speaks over it, so it cannot be just her impression again.*

JULIA. I will show you Harry.

HENRY. Are there bees here?

JULIA. I am the swarm and the hive and the bees and the honey. Bury yourself in me, this hive without stings. Practique moved between the empty hives, tall and dark and glittering with his million wings. Our skins touched and the bees flowed over us in friendship.

HENRY. Your skin seems made of wings and velvet. It rings like a living gong that you touch while it is still sounding.

JULIA. I am like that everywhere, Harry . . . inside, deep as flowers, deep as the sun turning to flowers turning to bees . . .

The bee-hum increases to an intolerable level, grows and breaks into the lovers' cries. Pause and silence. Breathing.

JULIA. That is our religion, Harry.

Pause.

This is what we have all seen.

Pause.

It is the vision of earth, Gaia, seen through me, seen through the bees.

HENRY. I believe you.

Pause.

JULIA. There is no death.

HENRY. I believe you.

JULIA. Only transformation.

HENRY. You? How could you, a mortal woman . . .

JULIA. Us, Harry.

HENRY. Us? Who else is here?

JULIA. Only the girls. Jennie and Anne.

HENRY. The girls.

There is pleasant light laughter from the other girls, a little humming.

JULIA. Harry, what is it? The flight is for us, equally. Two bodies could not do all we have done. We shared you.

HENRY. Share! This is not love! It is an orgy!

JENNIE. Men often feel a reaction after the vision.

HENRY. Vision! Imposition! Hallucination. I thought it happened because you loved me.

JULIA. So I do, yet I hardly know you. Jennie and Anne love you, though you have hardly exchanged a word with them.

HENRY. Four of us! Isn't there a less complicated way of seeing your truth?

JULIA. I'm afraid not. There are so many millions in the world. All are capable of it.

HENRY. No wonder your church — correction: 'hive' — came to a bad end.

JULIA. This was not the reason that happened. Here, you took the full charge of our longing. It is so long since we have had a candidate. We feel we have conceived from you.

HENRY. Longing! I call it wish-fulfillment. Candidate, indeed. I came looking for the explanation to a mystery.

JULIA. We have shown you the mystery. There is no explanation for what happens when love is made. You have taken your oath.

HENRY. And you made a promise. I wanted a different kind of fact. This bed is too sweet, too honied. I want to know where the man himself, Practique, has gone.

JENNIE. How do you know he isn't here with us, all the time?

Quiet laughter.

JULIA. Paul Masterson, Practique's friend, will tell you, now you have taken your oath. We will tell you where to find him.

HENRY. What's to prevent me telling all I know?

JENNIE. Nobody will believe you.

JULIA. You must kiss us goodbye.

Kissing, and a faint dying hum.

HENRY. Will love-making ever be like that again?

JULIA. It is always like that, whether you know it or not.

HENRY. What did they call you, the queens, the women who gave initiation?

JENNIE. They called us sometimes *suvasinis*, flowers, the sweet-smelling ones.

JULIA. But most often they called us *Melissai* . . .

HENRY. *Melissai*. What does it mean?

JULIA. It means 'Honies'.

Pause.

JAMES. Mr Masterson will see you, Sir. We are expecting the Doctor. Might I ask you to be prepared for his — affliction? He is a martyr to hives — a form of extreme nettlerash. Visitors are often startled by his appearance, and he prefers to forget it, as far as he can. He has his good days and his bad days.

HENRY. Is this a good day or a bad day — may I know your name?

JAMES. James, Sir. It is a good day. On a bad day I could not let you in at all. Mr Masterson creates a very powerful atmosphere around him, Sir, on a bad day.

HENRY. Is that because of his religion?

JAMES. I could not say, Sir. On bad days he does pray, very loud, with a kind of buzzing or humming. Do you see this crack here?

HENRY. What a shame! A beautiful mirror covering the whole wall and a jagged crack right down it!

JAMES. We do not keep mirrors in the rooms my master frequents, as that will remind him of his appearance. This room is kept for visitors. The Master must have taken a wrong turning. I found him in here, looking at himself in the mirror, and buzzing, Sir, buzzing so loud that the ornaments rattled and the chandelier shook. Suddenly a great crack ran down the mirror and split his reflection in half.

HENRY. This appearance of his. You say he is swollen.

JAMES. Yes, Sir, it is the hives. It is urticaria, a nettlerash, as though he had been rolling in them, or had been stung by bees. Sometimes his eyelids are so swollen that he cannot see at all. He sits with great fingers like sausages, propped on his chair like a great drowned corpse . . .

HENRY. Steady man . . . I wonder you stay, if you feel like that.

JAMES. It is my job, Sir. I am his nurse as well as his valet. (*Buzzer.*) He is ready to see you now . . .

Fade out.

Fade in.

PAUL. Come in, Dr Desmond. I'm afraid I cannot see you too well . . .

HENRY. I'm not . . .

PAUL. No, not too early. Not at all. I look forward to these sessions so much . . . hypnosis, or relaxation. I know you chaps prefer to call it the relaxation response nowadays, but you and I know it is the same old magic, don't we Doctor?

HENRY. The doctor is . . .

PAUL. Yes, quite ready, I'm sure. But I would prefer you not to use your passes or your whirling light, today. I am so . . . swollen, Doctor, so tense with pressure, that the slightest touch would be an agony. Your voice will be entirely sufficient. Look, it is as you taught me, I count to ten and I am already asleep. 1 . . . 2 . . . 3 . . . 4 . . .

HENRY. There is a misunderstanding. I am not . . .

PAUL. No, I have understood perfectly. My Master and I had such exercises. I have learnt your method. 5 . . . 6 . . . 6 . . . 7 . . .

HENRY (aside). I might as well let him go ahead, if he thinks I am the doctor, and I can find out what I need this way.

PAUL. 9 . . . 10. I am asleep, Dr Desmond, asleep and remembering.

HENRY. You are asleep.

PAUL. Asleep and awake at once, and going deeper with each breath.

HENRY. Deeper, and deeper.

PAUL. Oh this skin swollen with my guilt.

HENRY. Your Master, Practique, where is he now?

PAUL. Ah, this is my guilt, and my murder.

HENRY. But you can think of it now, and thinking of it will make you well. I take you back to Number Six, Stainton Square. It is a brilliant occasion, you are the right hand man, the St Paul of Master Practique. Do you love your Master?

PAUL. I hated him, and now I shall never be rid of him.

HENRY. Think back to that time, the great hall bright with the beeswax candles, light upon light reflected in the beeswax-polished panels and flooring, the years roll away.

PAUL. One of the bees had stung me in the mouth. He told me it was a sign I was not to preach that day, but to listen to him and write his testament. This is the night he preaches his great bee-sermon before the music is played that has been written for him, the great Mass. There he stands in his amber and gold, with his long cape of wings, and his fellow-men swarm to him like bees to drink the honey of his voice. He hummed and buzzed in the way that made obedience, and we were silent. The hum seemed to come from the entire surface of his body, which was impossible without the bees themselves. It filled the hall. Then, suddenly, ah . . .

HENRY. Deeper and deeper, steadier and steadier . . .

PAUL. . . . the hum deepened and seemed to sweep about the hall, and our five thousand heads turned from side to side watching the invisible swarm which having circled once, twice, thrice, swept right through the curtains at the back of the stage and silence fell.

HENRY. See into the past, deeper and deeper . . .

PAUL. I swear it was his soul flying. We buzzed and hummed with excitement and then fell silent as the minutes passed, our master tall and still on the great stage. He had preached his bee-sermon. What would happen next? Would he not return directly, open his eyes, and show us all how to leave our bodies like an invisible swarm of bees, to return and resurrect? Practique stood stiffly there still. Heads began to turn towards me, to comment, to intervene. I suppose three quarters of an hour had passed when I got up from my seat and approached the figure on the stage.

HENRY. Deeper and deeper, closer and closer.

PAUL. My Master's face was wet, with tears, I thought. As I got closer I saw that his eyes were not closed, they were strangely clouded over. I looked into them. It was as though the clear surfaces had crystallised. I touched his cheek. The tears were sticky. I put my finger to my mouth. There was a superb sweetness on it, like a magnificent honey. I touched his hand, which was raised in benediction. Ah me, it was as cold as wax.

HENRY. Deeper and deeper, no fear in these depths.

PAUL. Then I touched his hand and my hand was shaking, and it knocked against his folded little finger. It broke off like a brittle thing, and I just caught it in my two hands.

HENRY. You must be steady, you are there, in the great hall, deeper and deeper.

PAUL. And honey seeped from the broken finger in a long shining string. Half knowing what I was doing and half not knowing, I clapped my hand to my mouth and popped in the morsel of little finger . . .

HENRY. More and more relaxed . . .

PAUL. . . . and I tasted it and it was heavenly and I swung round to all our people and I shouted out, 'Oh, Practique — he is *delicious*!'

HENRY. Deeper and deeper . . .

PAUL. And they came in their ranks, out of their seats, and came tumbling on to the stage plucking and picking at their Master all in their velvet like an avalanche of bees and in thirty seconds I swear . . .

HENRY. Deeper and deeper . . .

PAUL. There was no Master. He had gone so fast that not a crumb or drop of honey was left. They sucked his empty clothes until all trace was gone of the delicious honeycomb he had become. I looked round and they were all smiling. As I looked the smiles disappeared and I saw there terror, and unsatisfied greed that looked at me and looked at each other. And I looked into my heart and saw there what I saw also on those other faces, that I had loved my master best sinking my teeth into that fragile comb which burst with delirious sweetness into my mouth . . .

HENRY. Deeper and deeper . . .

PAUL. . . . and that a part of me had gone for ever, and that I had swallowed the font of honey, the source itself, and that deep within I was swelling with its unendurable sweetness, of which there could never be enough . . .

HENRY. Your face is sticky. I touch it. It is honey.

PAUL. That is he . . .

HENRY. But it is pouring out of your eyes. Out of your mouth.

PAUL. Ah, detestable sweetness. I spit it out. I retch it out.

HENRY. It is pouring out of you, Masterson, all that honey festering for years is pouring out of you, leaving you awake with your sharp and rational hatred which is your true self, and hypnotism or no, you are shrinking, Mr Masterson; look, man, you are no longer swollen with sweetness; let me take you by the hand . . .

Fade out, fade in.

. . . to the other room and the great mirror. Look at yourself! Open your slender eyelids, 10,9,8,7,6,5, . . . James, your master is himself again.

JAMES. Dr Desmond has phoned, Sir, and says he will be late.

HENRY. No matter — we don't need him now, 4,3,2,1, . . . Mr Masterson, Paul, you are yourself again!

Slight pause.

PAUL. And who might *you* be?

HENRY. That doesn't matter. I am a pilgrim, and I have come to the end of my search. I have seen how the gods ruin men in different ways. You lost your Master ten years ago. I have just found him. And he may ruin me, as it seems good to him.

PAUL. James, who is this intruder? I gave express orders that no-one but my doctor was to be admitted. Please show him to the door. And then you can pack your own bags. I no longer need a nurse. You are fired.

JAMES. Quite your old self, Sir, quite your old self.

Fade out.

Fade in to the bee-loud garden of the first scene.

HENRY. Violence, sensuality, greed and harshness. They all became
what they were. Yet I feel I have learnt from these people. And
Master Practique himself, was he the only good man among them?
He became what flesh and blood were never intended to be, food for
the masses, honey-cake for the five thousand. Could any of that
congregation have got more than a scrap of him? And yet the hum is
here, still, in your garden, where it all began for me. Why was that
man broken to pieces? Did it leave anything behind but mourning,
did any of them truly fulfil themselves?

BEEKEEPER. Perhaps the librarian, putting his thoughts in order. Perhaps
you will, having merely been brushed by those wings. Do you see, men
have always felt this way about their gods. They are too dangerous.
They must be torn to pieces. The ancients sang their mourning song
to their god Dionysus Zagreus, just as you have. Why is he so strong,
and yet so weak? But, do you hear? Listen. The Master is still in the
flowers, the bees. Sweetness and light gather for another assault, the
honey gathers until it is too heavy, and heaven cannot hold it. Listen,
he is putting himself together again, until the next time, the next trial.

HENRY. That sound is still there, still underneath everything. Let me just
try that note (*He hums.*) It is a little like this, the sound, a little like
this (*He hums.*)

Bee-noise for forty seconds.

BEYOND THE PALE

by William Trevor

William Trevor was born in Mitchelstown, County Cork, in 1928, and spent his childhood in provincial Ireland. He attended a number of Irish schools and later Trinity College, Dublin. He is a member of the Irish Academy of Letters. His many books include *The Old Boys* (Hawthornden Prize), *The Boarding-House*, *The Love Department*, *The Day We Got Drunk on Cake*, *Mrs Eckdorf in O'Neill's Hotel*, *Miss Gomez and the Brethren*, *The Ballroom of Romance and Other Stories*, *Elizabeth Alone*, *Angels at the Ritz* (winner of the Royal Society of Literature Award in 1975), *The Children of Dynmouth* (Whitbread Award), *Lovers of Their Time* and *Other People's Worlds*. In 1976 he received the Allied Irish Bank's prize and in 1977 was awarded the CBE in recognition of his valuable services to Literature. Besides *Beyond the Pale*, he has written five other plays for radio. William Trevor lives in Devon, is married and has two sons.

Beyond the Pale was first broadcast on BBC Radio 3 on 8th July 1980. The cast was as follows:

MILLY	Prunella Scales
CYNTHIA	Sylvia Coleridge
STRAFE	Maurice Denham
DEKKO	Jonathan Scott
MR MALSEED	Michael Spice
MRS MALSEED	Penelope Lee
KITTY	Sheila McGibbon
WAITRESS/VOICE BY THE SEA	Maggie Shevlin
MAN'S VOICE	Michael McKnight
BOY	Jonathan Furphy
GIRL	Jennifer Wright

Director: Robert Cooper

Fade up the sound of the sea: neither a tranquil lapping of waves nor the fury of a storm. The sea sounds ordinary on a pleasant day. In the distance seagulls cry. MILLY's voice begins over these sounds. Very gradually they fade away to nothing.

MILLY (*as narrator*). I've always kept a diary on holiday, the writing on the left-hand side, snapshots pasted in opposite. I do it for the memories really, not that I'm a sentimental person, but it's nice to look back once in a while. The other thing is, I like to tell the truth: no bones about it, no hiding things away. What happens, happens. I have a way of saying, and I jot it all down. But these particular pages are really very different because events took over, which I believe, in retrospect, is the best way of describing what occurred. Afterwards, in fact, I discovered that this time I hadn't jotted down a single word. Nor were there any snapshots.

Long pause.

We always went to Ireland in June. Ever since the four of us began to go on holidays together, in 1965 it must have been, we had spent the first fortnight of the month at Glencorn Lodge Hotel in Co. Antrim. Perfection, as Dekko put it once, and none of us disagreed. It's a Georgian house by the sea, not far from the village of Ardbeag. It's quite majestic in its rather elegant way, a garden running to the very edge of a cliff, its long rhododendron drive — or avenue, as they say in Ireland. The English couple who bought the house in the early sixties, the Malseeds, have had to build on quite a bit but it's all been discreetly done, the Georgian style preserved throughout. Figs grow in the gardens, and apricots, and peaches in the greenhouses which old Mr Saxton presides over. He's Mrs Malseed's father actually. They brought him with them from Surrey, and their Dalmatians, Charger and Snooze.

It was Strafe who found Glencorn for us. He'd come across an advertisement in *The Lady* in the days when the Malseeds still felt the need to advertise. 'How about this?' he said one evening at the end of the second rubber, and then read out the details. We had gone away together the summer before, to a hotel that had been recommended on the Costa del Sol, but it hadn't been a success because the food was so appalling. 'We could try this Irish one,' Dekko suggested cautiously, which is what eventually we did.

The four of us have been playing bridge together for ages, Dekko, Strafe, Cynthia and myself. They call me Milly, though strictly speaking my name is Dorothy Milson. Dekko picked up his nickname at school, Dekko Deakin sounding rather good I dare say. He's tall and gangling, always immaculately suited, a beaky face beneath mousy hair in which flecks of grey add a certain distinction. Dekko has money of his own and though he takes out girls who are half his age he has never managed to get round to marriage. The uncharitable might say that he has a rather gormless laugh, but he's kind at heart. Dekko and Strafe were at school together, which must be why we all call Strafe by his surname: Major R.B. Strafe he is, the initials standing for Robert Buchanan. With the exception of Cynthia of course, we're of an age, the four of us, all in the early fifties: the prime of life, so Dekko insists. We live quite close to Leatherhead, where the Malseeds were before they decided to make the change from Surrey to Co Antrim. Quite a coincidence we always think.

At Glencorn Lodge the Malseeds are in the prime of life also. She dresses beautifully, differently every day, and changing of course in the evening. She has smooth grey hair which she once told me she entirely looks after herself, and she almost always wears a black velvet band in it. Her face is well made up, and for one who arranges so many vases of flowers and otherwise has to use her hands she manages to keep them marvellously in condition. Her fingernails are varnished a soft pink, and a small gold bangle always adorns her right wrist, a wedding present from her husband. He's rather shorter than she is, brown as a berry in a Donegal tweed suit.

Fade up the sound of the hall of Glencorn Lodge. MRS MALSEED *greets her newly arrived guests.*

MALSEED. Well, well, well. A hundred thousand welcomes.

MRS MALSEED. How very nice to see you all again.

MILLY. Oh, it *is* good to be back. What marvellous sweet-peas! I could bask in that scent for ever.

MALSEED. Good trip Major?

STRAFE. Not a worry all the way.

DEKKO. Calm as a puddle.

MRS MALSEED. The wretched boat sailed an hour early last week. Quite a little band were left stranded at Stranraer.

STRAFE (*laughing*). Catching the tide, I dare say?

MRS MALSEED. They caught a rocket from me. A couple of old dears were due with us on Tuesday and had to spend the night in some awful Scottish lodging-house. It nearly finished them.

Laughter.

MALSEED (*raising his voice*). Arthur!

ARTHUR. Sir.

MALSEED. Now, let's see what rooms you're in.

MRS MALSEED. Rose. Geranium. Hydrangea. Fuchsia.

MALSEED. Bags in from the car, Arthur. And then Rose, Geranium, Hydrangea, Fuchsia.

ARTHUR. Sir.

MRS MALSEED (*raising her voice*). Kitty! She's only in the dining-room and I know she'd just like to say hullo. (*Louder than before:*) Kitty!

DEKKO (*calling after* ARTHUR). I'll give you a hand with the luggage, Arthur.

ARTHUR. Oh, not at all, sir, not at all. I'll have it all up in no time and we can sort it out then.

STRAFE. Everything in the boot, Arthur.

ARTHUR. Surely, sir, surely.

MILLY (*making a lot out of this greeting*). Hullo, Kitty.

KITTY. Welcome back, ma'am. Welcome back, Major Strafe, Mr Deakin. And Mrs Strafe, ma'am. Sure, aren't you all looking younger? Ten years younger.

Laughter. When it dies down MILLY's *voice is earnest.*

MILLY. It's lovely to be back, Kitty. It really is.

KITTY. It's great to have you, ma'am.

Fade out.

Fade up the sound of the sea.

MILLY (*as narrator*). Nothing had changed. Kitty was the same old card; she's been with the Malseeds since they began. Arthur, who doubles as porter and odd-job man, had our suitcases sorted out in no time. Arthur's quite old, with a beaten, fisherman's face and short grey hair. He wears a green baize apron and a white shirt with an imitation silk scarf tucked into it at the neck. The scarf's an idea of Mrs Malseed's and one appreciates the effort.

Hold the sound of the sea, though a little more distant, as heard from MILLY's *bedroom.*

There's a knock at the door.

MILLY. Come in.

ARTHUR. I think maybe this is your cardigan, Mrs Milson. You left it on the hall desk.

MILLY. Oh Arthur, you are a dear. Thank you so much.

ARTHUR. No bother at all, madam.

MILLY. Let me find my handbag. Just a moment, Arthur. It's been quite a year for you, has it? No . . . ah . . . ?

Sound effect: she is now rooting for a coin in her handbag.

ARTHUR. Nothing like that whatsoever, Mrs Milson. Well, we never really, not at Ardbeag. No, it's mainly been the new annexe. Eight lovely rooms, doubles or singles, it doesn't matter which. All February and March it took me to decorate them, each of them different, lilac, mauve, pale green, pale orange, stone grey, stone brown — oh, thank you very much, Mrs Milson.

MILLY. I'll probably stroll over and look at it before dinner.

ARTHUR. I could show you into the rooms, some time when the guests are out.

MILLY. Oh no, I don't think —

ARTHUR. No bother at all, Mrs Milson. Cheerio now.

MILLY. Cheerio, Arthur.

The door closes behind him. MILLY *returns to the window and the view.*

Bring up the sound of the sea a little closer.

MILLY (*as narrator*). I was glad there'd been no trouble, because of course you never know. We'd come to adore County Antrim, its glens and coastline, Rathlin Island and Tievebulliagh. Since we first got to know it we'd all four fallen hopelessly in love with every variation of this remarkable landscape. People in England thought us mad of course: they see so much of the troubles on television that it's naturally difficult for them to realise that most places are just as they've always been. Yet coming as we did, taking the road along the coast, through Ballygally, it was impossible to believe that somewhere else the unpleasantness was going on. We had our walks and our drives, tweed to buy in Cushendall, Strafe's and Dekko's fishing day when Cynthia and I just sat on the beach, our visit to the Giant's Causeway and the one to Donegal which meant an early start and taking pot luck for dinner somewhere. We'd never seen a thing, nor even heard people talking about incidents that might have taken place. It's true that after a particularly nasty carry-on a few winters ago we did consider finding somewhere else, in Scotland perhaps, or Wales. But as Strafe put it at the time, we felt we owed a certain loyalty to the Malseeds and indeed to everyone we've come to know round about, people who'd always been glad to welcome us back. It seemed silly to lose our heads and when we returned the following summer we knew immediately we'd been right.

The sound of the sea, gentle at first, now becomes noisier, waves crashing through the rocks, wind. Cease abruptly, just as the sound becomes sinister.

Fade in the after-dinner lounge. MILLY, STRAFE, CYNTHIA *and* DEKKO *are playing bridge.*

STRAFE. Spades. Spades, Cynthia.

CYNTHIA. What?

STRAFE. Spades were led, dear. Diamonds are trumps.

CYNTHIA. Oh dear, I'm sorry.

DEKKO *laughs loudly.*

DEKKO. Doesn't worry us, eh, Milly?

MILLY. Cynthia's tired.

CYNTHIA. No, no, not at all. No, please —

STRAFE. Yes, I think we should call it a day.

DEKKO (*laughing again*). Can't say I'm exactly fresh as a daisy myself.

CYNTHIA. I'm so sorry —

STRAFE. Never mind, dear, never mind. Let's have a nightcap, eh? Cynthia? Milly?

CYNTHIA. No, not for me, thanks.

MILLY. I think I'd rather like a little Chartreuse. If I may, Strafe.

STRAFE (*calling out*). Arthur!

CYNTHIA. Perhaps I am sleepy. I think I'll just go to bed.

ARTHUR. Sir?

STRAFE. Bushmills and soda for my good self. One yellow Chartreuse for Mrs Milson. Cointreau for Mr Deakin. Right Dekko?

DEKKO. Absolutely.

ARTHUR. Straight away, Major.

MILLY. You never do manage to sleep on the boat, do you, dear?

CYNTHIA. I'm afraid not.

MILLY. I'm out like a light myself. The salt in the air, I think.

STRAFE. You run along, old girl.

CYNTHIA. I think I will. Good night.

STRAFE. 'Night old girl.

MILLY. 'Night, dear.

DEKKO. Brekky at nine, Cynth. (*He gives his laugh.*)

Bring up the murmur of the after-dinner lounge. Then fade it as MILLY *speaks.*.

MILLY (*as narrator*). There was a French family in what the Malseeds call the After-Dinner Lounge, two little girls and their parents, and a honeymoon couple, and the Uprichards, who'd occupied the table next to ours in the dining-room and who had made themselves known to us: an elderly couple from Guildford, quite nice they seemed. There were some pleasant Americans, and a man on his own. Of course there'd been other people at dinner because Glencorn Lodge is always full in June and from where we sat now, by one of the big windows of the lounge, we could see their shadows in the fading dusk, strolling about the lawns, a few returning along the cliff-path from the shore. We watched them for a moment, none of us commenting on Cynthia's tiredness because as a kind of unwritten rule we never comment on one another. We're four people who play bridge; the companionship it offers, and the holidays we have together, are all part of that. We share everything: the cost of petrol, the cups of coffee or drinks we have: we even each make a contribution towards the use of Strafe's car because it's always his we go on holiday in, a Rover it was on this occasion.

Strafe is on the stout side, I suppose you could say, with a gingery moustache and gingery hair, hardly touched at all by grey. He left the army years ago, I suppose because of me in a sense, because he didn't wanted to be posted abroad again. He's in the Ministry of Defence now.

I'm still quite pretty in my way, though nothing like as striking as Mrs Malseed, for I've never been that kind of woman. I've put on weight, but wouldn't have allowed myself to do so if Strafe hadn't kept saying he can't stand a bag of bones. I'm careful about my hair and, unlike Mrs Malseed, I have it very regularly seen to because if I don't it gets a salt and pepper look for one thing, which I hate.

My husband, Ralph, who died of food-poisoning when we were still quite young, used to say I wouldn't lose a single look in middle age, and to some extent that's true. We were still putting off having children when he died, which is why I haven't any. Then I met Strafe, which meant I didn't marry again.

Strafe of course is married to Cynthia. She's small and inclined to be dowdy, I suppose you'd say, without being untruthful or unkind. Not that Cynthia and I don't get on or anything like that, in fact we get on extremely well. It's Strafe and Cynthia who don't really hit it off, and I often think how much happier all round it would have been if Cynthia had married someone completely different, someone like Dekko in a way except that that mightn't quite have worked out either. The Strafes have two sons, both very like their father, both of them in the army. And the very sad thing is they think nothing of poor Cynthia.

Sound of after-dinner lounge continues.

ARTHUR. Now, Major.

STRAFE. Thank you, Arthur.

The glasses are placed on the table and ARTHUR *goes.*

DEKKO. Top of the mornin' to you.

STRAFE. Here's to Ireland.

MILLY. Cheers.

They drink.

STRAFE. Funny, being here on your own.

Silence. The other two don't know what he's talking about.

DEKKO. Not with you, Strafe. I mean, we never are.

STRAFE. That chap over there.

DEKKO. Oh, him. Commercial gent, I'd say.

STRAFE. Good heavens, no.

DEKKO. Fertilizers, I'd say. Kleeneze man?

STRAFE. You'd never get a rep in a place like this. Not even in Ireland.

DEKKO. You get them everywhere these days actually —

STRAFE. More like a builder. Speculative builder roaming about looking for bits of land.

Hold under sound effects.

MILLY (*as narrator*). I took no part in the argument. The lone man didn't much interest me. He was a red-haired man of about thirty, not wearing a tie, his collar open at the neck and folded back over the jacket of his blue serge suit. He was uncouth-looking, though it's a hard thing to say, not at all the kind of person one usually sees at Glencorn Lodge. He sat in the After-Dinner Lounge as he had in the dining-room, lost in some concentration of his own, as if calculating sums in his mind. There had been a folded newspaper on his table in the dining-room. It now reposed tidily on the arm of his chair, still unopened.

DEKKO. The odd thing is, he smiled at Cynthia.

STRAFE. At Cynthia? What d'you mean?

DEKKO (*laughs loudly*). He suddenly looked up and smiled when she walked past him on her way out. He'd been sitting there as if he never smiled in his life and then just as she was going by —

MILLY. Maybe Cynthia nodded good-night to him.

DEKKO. Something like that.

MR MALSEED *breezes up to them.*

MALSEED. No problems, Major? Settling in all right?

STRAFE. Fine, thank you.

DEKKO. Absolutely.

MILLY. That chicken cacciatora was delicious, Mr Malseed.

MALSEED. Yes, McBride's expanding his repertoire a bit this season.
I'll be interested to see how you find his scallops in brandy cream.

MILLY. Oh, I adore scallops.

STRAFE. Who's that fellow over there, Mr Malseed? Chap with red hair?

MALSEED. I'm awfully sorry about that, Major. My fault entirely, a
booking that came over the phone.

STRAFE. Good heavens, not at all. Splendid-looking fellow. No, we
were just curious.

DEKKO. Kleeneze man I said, and was put in my place with a thud.
(*He gives a laugh.*)

MALSEED (*murmuring*). It's awfully difficult to tell on the phone and
we'd just had a cancellation in the annexe. He's only here for a night
but (*with a little laugh*) I can tell you I was in the dog-house when
he walked into the hall. Everything in a canvas bag with a broken
zip; got a lift with our French friends. Odd sort of fish, I dare say
you thought?

STRAFE. No, not at all. No, we didn't mean to be critical —

DEKKO. Takes all sorts, Mr Malseed. And a dreary old world it would
be if it didn't. (*He laughs again.*) My old dad used to say that, 'smatter
of fact. Whenever anyone commented on anyone else he'd just shake
his head slightly and say it took all sorts. Quite nice really.

MALSEED. Yes, of course. Well, I'll bid you goodnight. Mrs Strafe gone
on, has she, Major?

STRAFE. Yes, Cynthia's gone up.

MILLY. Good night, Mr Malseed.

DEKKO. 'Night.

STRAFE. 'Night.

Sound effects under MILLY'*s speech.*

MILLY (*as narrator*). Soon after that I went up myself, leaving the men
to enjoy another drink together. On holidays the Strafes always
occupy different rooms, and at home also. This time he was in
Geranium and she in Fuchsia. I was in Rose, and in a little while
Strafe would come to see me. He stays with her out of kindness,
because he fears for her on her own. He's a sentimental, good-hearted

man, easily moved to tears: he simply cannot bear the thought of Cynthia with no one to talk to in the evenings, with no one to make her life around. 'And besides,' he often says when he's being jocular, 'it would break up our bridge four.' Naturally we never discuss her shortcomings or in any way analyse the marriage, the unwritten rule that exists between the four of us seems to extend as far as that.

That night he slipped into my room after he'd had his drink with Dekko, and I was waiting for him as he likes me to wait, in bed but not quite undressed. He has never said so, but I know that that is something Cynthia would never understand in him, or ever attempt to comply with. My husband Ralph, of course, would not have understood either; poor old Ralph would have been shocked.

Fade up, faintly, the sound of the sea, as heard from the bedroom.

MILLY (*as narrator*). We lay there together with the window wide open both of us quite intensely happy.

Sound of the sea: the waves, gentle at first, then become rougher, until the sound is like a continuing explosion. What was just becoming sinister in this sound before is now identified: beneath the roar of wind and sea, there is the sound of human anguish. A man's voice cries and moans. There's a spluttering, as if he's drowning. A woman's voice, terrified, repeatedly cries 'No'.

Cease all sound abruptly.

Fade up morning birdsong, then the rattle of dishes: breakfast on the terrace of Glencorn Lodge. DEKKO is telling an Irish joke.

DEKKO. It must have been . . . late at night, I dare say, of course he'd had a few. Anyway, he'd just put the receiver down, having told his wife he'd been delayed and received a hefty portion of tongue pie for his pains.

MILLY. Coffee.

STRAFE. Thank you Milly.

DEKKO (*in thick drunken Irish accents*). 'Well, how in de name of God d'you get out of dis place?' he said. 'Sure isn't it all glass?' Well, he stood there for a minute, cogitating on his predicament and then he picked up the receiver and dialled 999. 'Which service do you require?' the voice said. 'Well, bedad I'm not sure.' he said. 'I've got locked inside a telephone box. Could you tell me dis,' he said, 'is der an exit to a telephone box at all at all?' 'Which service do you require, sir?' the operator repeated. 'Sure amn't I telling you, dear? I came into a telephone box to make a call to de wife and I can't get out. Which way are you facing, sir? Face the instrument, sir: the door's behind you.'

DEKKO laughs loudly. There's the rattle of STRAFE's newspaper.

MILLY. More coffee, Cynthia?

CYNTHIA. Thank you.

STRAFE's *newspaper rattles again. He reads from it.*

STRAFE. Long sunny spells, continuing dry. What could be nicer?

MILLY. Certainly more promising than last year.

DEKKO. They had to send a police car in the end. 'It must have been locked on de outside,' our hero said. 'Sorry to trouble you, officer.'

DEKKO's *laughter. The two women obediently join in, though without much enthusiasm.*

STRAFE. We thought of walking over to Ardbeag this morning, dear. Dekko and I want to fix up our fishing day with Henry O'Reilly.

CYNTHIA. I think I'll sit in the garden for a while.

MILLY. Poor Cynthia's still tired.

CYNTHIA. No, no, I slept marvellously. No, I'll enjoy seeing how the garden is this year. Then I'll settle down with my book in that little nook by the magnolias.

DEKKO. Poor old sausage.

CYNTHIA. I'll be perfectly all right.

STRAFE. She likes to mooch, you know.

Hold sound effects under.

MILLY (*as narrator*). She reads too much, I always think. You often see her putting down a book with the most melancholy look in her eyes, which can't be good for her. She's an imaginative woman, I suppose you would say, and of course her habit of reading so much is often useful on our holidays. Over the years she has read her way through dozens of Irish guide-books. 'That's where the garrison pushed the natives over the cliffs,' she once remarked on a drive. 'Those rocks are known as the Maidens,' she pointed out on another occasion. She has led us to places of interest which we had no idea existed: Garron Tower on Garron Point, the mausoleum at Bonamargy, the Devil's Backbone. As well as which, Cynthia is extremely knowledgeable about all matters relating to Irish history. Again, she has read endlessly: biographies and autobiographies, long accounts of the centuries of battling and politics there've been. There's hardly a town or a village we ever pass through that doesn't have significance for Cynthia, although I'm afraid her impressive fund of information doesn't always receive the attention it deserves. Not that Cynthia ever minds; it doesn't seem to worry her when no one listens. My own opinion is that she'd have made a much better job of her relationship with Strafe and her sons if she could have somehow been a bit more characterful.

Crossfade under the sea.

Anyway, when we'd finished breakfast we left her in the garden and proceeded down the cliff path to the shingle beneath. I was wearing slacks and a blouse with the arms of a cardigan looped round my neck in case it turned chilly: the outfit was new, specially bought for the holiday, in shades of tangerine. Strafe never cares how he dresses and of course she doesn't keep him up to the mark: that morning, as far as I remember, he wore rather shapeless corduroy trousers, the kind men sometimes garden in, and a navy-blue fisherman's jersey. Dekko as usual was a fashion plate: a pale green linen suit with pleated jacket pockets, a maroon shirt open at the neck, revealing a medallion on a fine gold chain. We didn't converse as we crossed the rather difficult shingle, but when we reached the sand Dekko told another of his Irish jokes and then started up about some girl or other, someone called Juliet who had apparently proposed marriage to him just before we'd left London.

Fade up the sound of the sea and footsteps, then fade to the background as DEKKO *speaks.*

DEKKO. I said I'd think about it while I was over here actually.

STRAFE. Send her a telegram from Ardbeag. 'Still, thinking' say.

DEKKO *laughs.*

MILLY. It's time you were married, Dekko.

STRAFE. Every couple of days or so send another one with the same message.

Both DEKKO *and* STRAFE *laugh like schoolboys.*

DEKKO. Remember the telegram Thrive Major sent Cows?

STRAFE (*laughing*). Oh, my gosh, I do.

DEKKO. In the picture, Milly? Remember old A.D. Cowley-Stubbs, keen misogynist? Thrive Major, always a bit of a wag, sent him a wire: Darling regret three months gone Rowena. Cows used to have coffee sessions in his study on Thursday evenings, five or six of his favourites sitting round discussing Sophocles. 'Come!' he called out in a way he had when there was a knock on the door, 'Telegram for you, sir,' Thrive announced, having managed to collect it from the messenger. When he read it, it seems Cows went white as a bath.

STRAFE. I was there myself as a matter of fact. The poor old beggar collapsed into his armchair and I remember Warrington P.J. picking up the telegram and glancing at it. He said afterwards he thought he'd better in case someone had died, although frankly I could never entirely see the logic of that. Thrive Major just stood there, not moving a muscle.

DEKKO. Warrington, P.J. —

STRAFE. Warrington P.J. immediately burst out laughing, couldn't help himself. He was cut up about it later and apologised fairly profusely to the Cow. Unfortunately everyone else was beginning to giggle also because somehow or other the telegram got passed around.

DEKKO. Rowena was a maid who'd been sacked a couple of terms ago, Milly. Known as the Bicycle.

STRAFE. People actually believed it. They actually believed that Cowley-Stubbs and the Bicycle had had some doings together. Years later, I believe, it was even suggested that the adopted child of the boxing instructor's wife was actually the progeny of this extraordinary union. Did you ever hear that, Dekko?

DEKKO. Indeed I did. In fact it was Thrive Major who told me, claiming he'd started the rumour himself, through his younger brother.

STRAFE. Thrive didn't care for poor Cows because of a dispute over a table-lamp, Milly. Cows broke it when giving Thrive six of the best and sent the bill to Thrive's father.

DEKKO. On the grounds that if Thrive hadn't shifted his position while the blows were falling the accident wouldn't have happened.

Both men laugh, and MILLY *eventually joins in their merriment, though in a more restrained manner. Bring up sound effects through their laughter and, hardly noticeable at first, the sound of the sea. Again there is the moaning of someone in distress. A woman, terrified, repeatedly shouts 'No!' There are four revolver shots. Fade, slowly, the tempestuous sea sound: it is now a gentle lapping. There are children's voices distant and almost lost beneath the sea sound.*

GIRL. Where are you? Where are you?

BOY. I'm miles away. I'm miles away. (*His voice is mocking, though affectionately and happily so.*)

GIRL. No, please. Please.

BOY. I'm in the woods. I'm by the cottage. I've gone to the white farm-house. I'm by the spring.

GIRL (*beseechingly*). Tell me. Please tell me.

BOY. I'm here beside you.

Bring up the sound of the sea. A man drowns, moaning and spluttering.

Through this, bring up MILLY's *voice.*

MILLY (*as narrator*). I never mind listening when they drift back to the days of old Cows their housemaster. They share a simple humour. All the way to Ardbeag Strafe kept insisting that Dekko should send regular telegrams to this girl called Juliet, to say he was still thinking about marriage with her. Sometimes when Dekko throws his head back to laugh I am reminded of an Australian bird I once saw on television, but for long years he has been a loyal friend to Strafe and for that a great deal must be forgiven. It's odd, the things you remember I don't think I'll ever forget the walk along the beach that morning, from Glencorn to Ardbeag. It seems right, in a way, that we were all three so jolly and getting on so well, jokes about schooldays and telegrams, a kind of happiness between us. When we arrived in Ardbeag we had coffee in the little cafe there and then Strafe and Dekko went to visit their friend Henry O'Reilly about their fishing day. None of us was thinking about Cynthia, of that I'm certain. We'd left her in the nook among the magnolias with her book, where she had clearly stated she wished to be. But looking back now it wasn't of course just with her book we'd left her: there was her silly imagination as well.

Sound has crossed back to the lapping of waves. Through this, the voices of the children.

BOY. I love you. I've fallen in love with you.

GIRL. Like they say in the films.

BOY. They kiss in the films.

GIRL. 'I love you, too,' they say.

BOY. The old films are best.

GIRL. I love you, too.

Bring up, louder, the lapping of waves: the voices are lost in it. Fade under the narration.

MILLY (*as narrator*). I bought postcards in Hamill's Stores, little views of the quay at Ardbeag and of the Glencorn cliffs and the lighthouse further around the coast, and of Warrior Rock. I bought cheap little trinkets in bog-oak and quite a nice pottery butter-dish, or perhaps an ashtray. I give things like that to Mrs Swann, who's my char, and I usually bring something small back for her daughter's children. Anyway, I had a long chat with Mr Hamill, who remembered me from other years. He gave me all the news of Ardbeag, how his cousin, whose garage had failed, was now in the mushroom business, how another cousin was thinking of going in for mink farming. I walked down to the quay and watched the fishermen unloading their catch. Then Strafe and Dekko arrived, full of Henry O'Reilly, who always insists that they have a glass of Bushmills with him. A shark had O'Reilly's right arm off a few years back, but he manages remarkably well with a hook. Like a lot of the people round here, he's quite a character, rather fond of his Bushmills I think. Strafe and Dekko had also been to the post office to send off Dekko's telegram, and as we strolled back to the hotel along the sands, the talk again turned to telegrams and in particular to the one dispatched to A.D. Cowley-Stubbs by Thrive Major. I really didn't mind a bit. Strafe recalled that the maid whose name had been taken in vain had in fact found herself in the family way, due to the attentions of a local publican. It was quite intriguing in a sense how the boy called Thrive had cunningly assembled all the facts: the maid's pregnancy, the later adopting of a child by the wife of the boxing instructor, the misogynistic character of Cowley-Stubbs. The boy moved them about to suit his own purposes, quite irrespective of the truth. I remarked as much and was told, which I could quite believe, that Thrive Major had been an extraordinary beggar. He'd ended up in Africa apparently, running some dubious mail-order concern. We laughed over all that, and over the telegram that already was on its way to the girl called Juliet. We were in the highest possible spirits as we clambered up the cliff path to the hotel lawns.

Bring up the sound of their footsteps, the exertion of the climb.

Then, still from a long way off, KITTY *calls to them. She comes running from the hotel to meet them.*

KITTY. Major Strafe! Major Strafe!

The three, having begun to walk across the lawn to the hotel, pause.

STRAFE. Whatever's the matter with her?

KITTY (*still some distance away*). Major! Mrs Milson!

Breathless, she arrives beside them. At first she can scarcely speak.

MILLY. Catch your breath, Kitty. Just take it calmly now.

KITTY. It's Mrs Strafe. (*Overcome for a moment by breathlessness.*) She needs looking after, Major.

MILLY (*as narrator*). The hotel in fact, was in a turmoil. Cynthia was in the hall, huddled in a chair. Mr Malseed was ashen-faced; his wife, in a forget-me-not dress, was limp. She left us standing there and in the middle of telling us what had happened Mr Malseed was summoned to the telephone. I could see through the half open door of his little office a glass of whisky or brandy on the desk and Mrs Malseed's bangled arm reaching out for it. Not for ages did we realise that it all had to do with the lone man whom we'd speculated about the night before.

CYNTHIA. He just wanted to talk to me. He sat with me by the magnolias.

MILLY. Dear, I think you should perhaps lie down.

STRAFE. Yes, come along, dear.

STRAFE *takes his wife's arm. All four move across the hall, to the stairs.* MR MALSEED *can be heard on the telephone in the office.*

MALSEED. Hullo, yes, yes, it is. Malseed here . . .

CYNTHIA. I couldn't stop him. From half-past ten until well after twelve. He had to talk to someone, he said.

They go upstairs. Fade sound under.

MILLY (*as narrator*). I could sense that Strafe and Dekko were thinking precisely the same as I was: that the red-haired man had insinuated himself into Cynthia's company by talking about himself and had then put a hand on her knee. Instead of simply standing up and going away Cynthia would have stayed where she was, embarrassed or tongue-tied, at any rate unable to cope. And when the moment came she would have turned hysterical. I could picture her screaming in the garden, running across the lawn to the hotel, and then the pandemonium in the hall. I could sense Strafe and Dekko picturing that also.

Sound effects: they are now entering CYNTHIA's *room.*

CYNTHIA. My God, it's terrible.

STRAFE. Try to tell us, Cynthia.

CYNTHIA. I was reading and suddenly he was there. He smiled at me, just a little, like he did last night after dinner. He'd picked me out: I knew that, I could see it in his eyes.

DEKKO. I noticed he smiled at you last night, Cynth. I said so to the others actually. 'He smiled at Cynth,' I said; I think they thought I was pulling their legs.

STRAFE (*quietly*). All right, Dekko, all right.

MILLY (*to* STRAFE). I think she should try to sleep.

STRAFE. Milly's right, dear. You'll feel much better after a little rest, and you can tell us about it then.

CYNTHIA. My God, how could I sleep?

DEKKO. Would you take one of my pills, Cynth?

CYNTHIA *begins to sob.*

STRAFE (*still quietly*). Yes, I think she would, Dekko.

DEKKO. Absolutely. (*He goes.*)

CYNTHIA. I wish I might never wake up. I wish I'd never been born into this awful world.

Fade sound effects under.

MILLY (*as narrator*). We made her lie down. Strafe and I stood on either side of her bed as she lay there with her shoes off, her rather unattractively cut plain blue dress crumpled and actually damp from her tears. I wanted to make her take it off and slip under the bedclothes in her petticoat but somehow it seemed all wrong, in the circumstances, for Strafe's wife to do anything so intimate in my presence. She was in a kind of daze, one moment making a fuss and weeping, the next just peering ahead of her, as if still frightened. Dekko returned with his pills and she took two obediently enough.

Bring up restaurant sounds. Lunch is being taken at Glencorn Lodge.

DEKKO. Poor old Cynth. Poor old sausage.

STRAFE. I can't make head or tail of it. Malseed appeared to have a couple of policemen in his office when we passed by.

MILLY. I honestly wouldn't have thought —

STRAFE. Of course not. No need for them whatsoever.

WAITRESS. Lobster bisque?

MILLY. For me please, and Mr Deakin.

STRAFE. I'm the crab cocktail.

WAITRESS. Thank you, sir.

MRS MALSEED *is hurrying across the dining room towards them.*

DEKKO. Of course it's secluded there in the magnolias. Easy enough for a chap —

MRS MALSEED. Major Strafe, I wonder if my husband might have a word with you in the office? I'm extremely sorry to interrupt your lunch but —

STRAFE. Of course, of course.

Together they cross the dining-room. MILLY *and* DEKKO *eat their soup in silence. Hold sound effects under narration.*

MILLY (*as narrator*). We just sat there, not even saying anything when the waitress came to clear away our soup-plates. Already both of us could feel that a storm in a teacup had been blown up out of all proportion, and we felt as well that there was nothing whatsoever we or Strafe or anyone else could do about it. Then Strafe returned and told us what had happened: after talking to Cynthia for more than two hours the man had walked down to the rocks and been drowned.

Sound effects: continue scene.

DEKKO. My God!

STRAFE. He left her where she was sitting among the magnolias and went down the cliff by a path no one ever uses, the other side of the hotel from where we were returning along the sands. But Cynthia, apparently, had gone to the cliff edge herself and stood there watching him struggling against the current.

MILLY. Stood there?

STRAFE. She apparently witnessed everything. The tide, you remember, was coming in this morning. By the time Arthur and Malseed reached the rocks it had begun to turn, leaving the corpse behind it. Malseed's impression was that the man had slipped in the seaweed of the rocks.

MILLY. How dreadful!

STRAFE. But Cynthia insisted the man drowned himself.

Silence.

MILLY. You mean, she says she watched him committing suicide?

STRAFE. Yes.

DEKKO. But, Strafe, why didn't —

STRAFE. There was no point in his living, she told the Malseeds, but I
imagine that's just her distress talking. The police want to see her
when she's recovered. I said she'd been given a couple of sleeping-pills.

Silence.

MILLY. I'm sorry, I simply don't understand this at all.

DEKKO. How could she possibly know at that distance if he slipped or
not? Those rocks are a very long way down.

STRAFE (*slowly, thoughtfully*). I suppose what she's thinking is that
after he'd tried something on with her he became depressed.

MILLY. Oh, but he could just as easily have lost his footing. He'd have
been on edge anyway, worried in case she reported him. What beats
me is why she didn't stand up the moment he began to paw her and
go straight to the Malseeds? Whatever's come over Cynthia?

DEKKO. Frightful kind of death, no matter how it came about. Frightful
for the Malseeds.

MILLY. I must say I didn't much care for the look of that man.

STRAFE. They've carted the body off. I think it's more or less the end
of the matter. Except for Cynthia's little chat with the police officers.
It's just routine, that, I understand.

DEKKO. It's shaken me up, I can tell you that.

STRAFE. We'll all feel better when we've had a bit of a lie down.

Fade sound effects.

MILLY (*as narrator*). After lunch we went to our rooms as we always do
at Glencorn Lodge, to rest for an hour. I took my slacks and blouse
off, hoping that Strafe would knock on my door, but he didn't and
of course that was understandable. Oddly enough I found myself
thinking of Dekko, picturing his long form stretched out in the room
called Hydrangea, his beaky face in profile on his pillow. The precise
nature of Dekko's relationship with these girls he picks up has always
privately intrigued me: was it really possible that somewhere in London
there was a girl called Juliet who was prepared to marry him for his not
inconsiderable money? Then I thought about the man with the red
hair, imagining him bothering Cynthia and then slipping on the seaweed.
I couldn't feel sorry for him because it's most unpleasant to be bothered
in that way. It served him right in a sense, that the accident had occurred.
It was only unfortunate that one of our party had been involved;
typical of Cynthia, I couldn't help thinking. I slept and dreamed that
Thrive Major and Warrington P.J. were running a post office in Africa,
sending telegrams to everyone they could think of, including Dekko's
friend Juliet. The Irishman in the telephone box was the red-haired man
and the telephone-box was in the sea, floating away into the distance.
Cynthia had been found dead among the magnolias and everyone was

waiting for Hercule Poirot to arrive. 'Promise me you didn't do it,' I whispered to Strafe, but when Strafe replied it was to say that Cynthia's body reminded him of a bag of old chicken bones.

Bring up the soft lapping of waves.

From a great distance come the voices of the two children.

GIRL. Where are you? Please tell me where you are.

BOY. Ahhh.

GIRL. Why do you tease me?

BOY. I'll never not love you they say in the films. You're prettier than Kim Novak . . .

The sound of the sea drowns the continuing voices. Crossfade to the tea lounge. DEKKO and MILLY are present. All around them other guests are having tea.

DEKKO (*breezily*). Yes, I think so. The full tea, eh, Milly? After all, we didn't manage much lunch in the end.

MILLY. Yes, please, Kitty.

KITTY. Very good, ma'am.

DEKKO. I imagine Major Strafe will have the full tea too, Kitty. Certainly Mrs Strafe will: poor dear, she missed lunch altogether.

KITTY. Very good, sir.

MILLY. She never eats much, you know. Here's Strafe now.

STRAFE *joins them and sits down.*

STRAFE. Well, I feel a very great deal better now.

DEKKO. Has Cynth —?

STRAFE. She was just beginning to wake up as I passed. I said where we'd be.

MILLY. I think the Malseeds are themselves again.

STRAFE. Yes. He asked me if I wouldn't mind driving Cynthia to the police station rather than have them returning here.

DEKKO. Understandable, that.

STRAFE. It should only take a couple of minutes apparently. We could perhaps go for a little drive afterwards, call in at that pub on the Ardbeag road for a quick one before dinner.

DEKKO. What a smart idea, Strafe! (*He laughs.*)

MILLY. I had the oddest of dreams. All about your school chums and a man in a telephone-box floating out to sea.

KITTY. Here we are then.

STRAFE. Thank you, Kitty.

Sound effect: the tray of tea is placed on the table between them.

MILLY. McBride hasn't lost his touch, I see. Those curranty scones are as light-looking as ever.

STRAFE. Ah, here's Cynthia.

Hold the tea lounge sound effects.

MILLY (*as narrator*). And here indeed she was. By the look of her she had simply pushed herself off her bed and come straight down. Her blue dress was even more cumpled than before. She hadn't so much as run a comb through her hair, her face was puffy and unpowdered. For a moment I really thought she was walking in her sleep.

Sound effects: continue scene.

STRAFE. Feeling better, dear?

DEKKO. Sit down, Cynth.

CYNTHIA. That man's dead. He was battered about like a cork. It only took five minutes.

STRAFE. You must try and forget it all, dear.

CYNTHIA. He told me a story I can never forget. I've dreamed about it all over again.

MILLY (*cheerfully*). I was just saying I had the oddest dream. On the way over to Ardbeag we were talking about telegrams — well, Dekko sending a telegram to this Juliet girl was how it all began —

CYNTHIA. 'D'you mind?' he said. 'D'you mind if I tell you a story about two children?' He didn't even know my name; nor I his.

MILLY. Strafe.

STRAFE. Oh, thank you. Story, dear?

CYNTHIA. The story of two children who rode away on their dilapidated bicycles from their city streets — from poverty and unhappiness, from the clutter and the quarrelling. He didn't speak of their two different homes, he didn't say if the bicycles had been stolen. But in my dream I saw the children clearly. Two children who fell in love.

STRAFE. Horrid old dream. Horrid for you, dear.

MILLY (*still cheerfully*). Mine was all about Thrive Major and Warrington P.J. You probably know, Cynthia, how they once —

CYNTHIA. A fragile thing she was, with depths of mystery in her wide brown eyes. Red-haired and freckled he was himself, thin as a rake in those days. They played a kind of hide and seek when they were here; Glencorn Lodge was derelict then. Odd to come back to, he said. Odd to sleep in a room called Japonica.

DEKKO. You've had a bit of a shock, old thing.

STRAFE. Most unpleasant.

DEKKO. You'll feel much better after a cup of tea.

STRAFE. Look, dear, if the chap actually interfered with you —

CYNTHIA (*suddenly shrill*). Why on earth should he do that?

Her shrillness causes a sudden silence in the tea lounge.

STRAFE. Shh, dear.

CYNTHIA. It was summer when they came here. Honeysuckle, he described. And Mother of Thyme. Although he didn't know the name of either.

Crossfade from tea lounge to the lapping of the waves. Then fade up the children's voices under.

GIRL. Where are you? Where are you?

BOY. I'm miles away. I'm miles away. (*His voice is mocking, though affectionately and happily so.*)

GIRL. No, please. Please.

BOY. I'm in the woods. I'm by the cottage. I've gone to the white farmhouse. I'm by the spring.

GIRL (*beseechingly*). Tell me. Please tell me.

BOY. I'm here beside you. I love you. I've fallen in love with you.

GIRL. Like they say in the films.

BOY. They kiss in the films.

GIRL. 'I love you, too,' they say.

BOY. The old films are best.

GIRL. I love you, too.

Crossfade back from the lapping of the waves to the buzz in the lounge.

CYNTHIA. At school there were the facts of geography and arithmetic. And the legends, of scholars and of heroes, of Queen Maeve and Finn Mac Cool. There was the coming of St Patrick to a heathen people. History was full of kings and high kings, of Silken Thomas and Wolfe Tone, the Flight of the Earls, the Siege of Limerick. Of battles and of murders.

Hold tea lounge sound effects under.

MILLY (*as narrator*). When Cynthia said that, it was impossible not to believe that the unfortunate events of the morning had touched her with some kind of madness. It seemed astonishing that she had walked into the tea lounge without having combed her hair, that out of the blue she had started on about two children. None of it made an iota of sense, and surely she could see that the nasty experience she'd had should not be dwelt upon? I offered her the plate of scones, hoping that if she began to eat she would stop talking. But she took no notice of my gesture.

Sound effect: continue scene.

CYNTHIA. Did she like needlework and cookery? Did she pick her heroes out of history?

STRAFE. Look, dear, I have to tell you not one of us knows what you're talking about.

CYNTHIA. I'm talking about a children's story. I'm talking about a girl and a boy who visited this place. He hadn't been back for years, but he returned last night, making one last effort to understand. And then he walked out into the sea.

MILLY. Cynthia, dear, drink your tea and why not have a scone?

CYNTHIA. They rode those worn-out bicycles through a hot afternoon gorgeously escaping. Can you feel all that? A newly surfaced road, the snap of chippings beneath their tyres? Dust from a passing car, the smell of tar?

STRAFE (*sighing*). No, no, we really cannot, dear.

CYNTHIA. They swam and sunbathed on the beach you walked along today. They went to a spring for water. There were no magnolias then. There was no garden, no neat little cliff paths to the beach. This place that is an idyll for us was an idyll for them too: the trees, the ferns, the wild roses near the water spring, the very sun and sea. There was a cottage lost in the middle of the woods: they sometimes looked for that. They played their game of hide and seek. People in a white farmhouse gave them milk.

Silence.

DEKKO. All's well that's over. There is that, Cynth.

Hold tea lounge acoustic under.

MILLY (*as narrator*). But Cynthia appeared to have drifted back into a daze, and I wondered if it could really be possible that the experience had unhinged her. Unable to help myself, I saw her led away from the hotel, helped into the back of a blue van, something like an ambulance.

Sound effect: continue scene.

CYNTHIA. Has it to do with their city streets? Or the history they learnt, he from his Christian Brothers, she from her nuns? History is unfinished in this island; long since it has come to a stop in Surrey.

STRAFE. Take it easy, dear.

DEKKO. We have to put it behind us, old Cynth.

CYNTHIA. Two hundred years after the birth of Christ the high kingship of Tara began; half a century later only the Gaelic of the ruling classes and the Latin of the Church were spoken. The Norsemen came; there has been bloodshed ever since. The Pope gave Ireland to Henry II in 1172. Did you know that? That the Pope actually gave a country to a king?

STRAFE (*sharply*). No, I don't think we did, dear.

CYNTHIA. The Mandevilles were powerful here among the glens we know and all along our coastal drive, a Norman family more Irish than the Irish. They changed their name to MacQuillan and ruled until their land was taken from them in 1603. Can you imagine our very favourite places bitter with that disaffection, with plotting and revenge, and the treacherous murder of Shane O'Neill the Proud? (*Pause.*) Confusion thickens, like convolvulus in a hedgerow. Chaos and contradiction and nice-sounding names: Finola MacDonnell, Malachy who wore the collar of gold that he won from the proud invader. The Carews of Carlow and of Cork, Richard FitzGilbert Clare, Walter de Burgo, Niall of the Nine Hostages. Sir Robert Devereux, Sir Charles Coote, Robert Emmet, Napper Tandy. O'Neill of the Fews. How easily they all trip off the tongue, these friends and enemies who are not even shadows now! (*Pause.*) The Battle of Vinegar Hill, the Battle of Callan, the Battle of Kinsale, the Battle of the Yellow Ford, the Battle of Glenmama, the Battle of Benburb, the Battle of the Pass of Plumes. The Statutes of Kilkenny. The Act of Settlement, the Act of Oblivion, the Act of Explanation, the Poor Relief Act, the Renunciation Act, the Act of Union, the Toleration Act. (*Pause.*) Beneath those pretty titles people were crushed, or starved, or died, while other people watched. A language was lost, a faith forbidden. Famine followed revolt, plantation followed that. But it was people who were stuck into the soil of other people's land, not forests of new trees; and it was greed and treachery that spread as a disease among all of them. No wonder unease still clings to these shreds of history and shots ring out in answer to the mockery of drums, no wonder the air is nervy with suspicion.

Silence.

DEKKO (*awkwardly*). What an awful lot you know, Cynth!

STRAFE (*equally awkwardly*). Cynthia's always been interested. Always had a first-rate memory.

CYNTHIA. Those children of the streets are part of the battles and the Acts, the blood that flowed around those nice-sounding names. The second time they came here the house was being rebuilt. There were concrete mixers and lorries drawn up on the grass, noise and scaffolding everywhere. They watched all through another afternoon and soon afterwards they went their different ways: their childhood was over, their love lost with their idyll. He became a dockyard clerk. She went to London, to work in a betting shop.

STRAFE. My dear, though it's interesting, everything you say, it hardly concerns us, you know.

CYNTHIA. No, of course not. Those children were degenerate, awful creatures: they must have been.

STRAFE (*sharply*). No one's saying that, my dear.

CYNTHIA. Their story should have ended there, he in the dockyards of Belfast, she recording bets. Their complicated childhood love should just have dissipated, as such love often does.

DEKKO. There was a chap — Gollsol, I think his name was. Remember him, Strafe, great big fellow? Romantic attachment for the daughter of one of the groundsmen. Married her ten years later, so someone said. Odd thing to do, eh? (*Hastily.*) Not that I'm saying it's the same, Cynth —

CYNTHIA (*speaks quietly, without emotion*). You none of you care. You sit there not caring that two people are dead.

MILLY. Two people, Cynthia?

CYNTHIA (*cries out, greatly upset suddenly*). For God's sake, I'm telling you! He killed her in a room in Maida Vale.

Silence.

MILLY. Dear, are you sure you're not muddling something up here? You've been upset, you've had a nightmare: don't you think your imagination, or something you've been reading —

CYNTHIA. Bombs don't go off on their own. Death does not just happen to occur in Derry and Belfast, in London and Amsterdam and Dublin, in Berlin and Jerusalem. There are people who are murderers. (*Pause.*) Those children became that.

Silence. MILLY *pours tea.*

In this peaceful place we drink our gin with Angustura bitters. There's lamb with rosemary, and Chicken Kief. A hundred thousand welcomes, Mr Malseed says; we play our bridge and buy our tweed. Thrive Major lightens the conversation and Warrington P.J. and A.D. Cowley-Stubbs. We laugh because a drunk is stupid in a telephone box. In Surrey, too, Thrive Major is talked about, the tricks he played a million years ago; jokes are told in Surrey, too; we hear of girls and marriage. In Surrey the horror's on the television screen, bland as a grey felt hat.

STRAFE (*sharply*). Please keep your voice down.

CYNTHIA. Flowers are everywhere in this hotel. Old Kitty's kind to us in the dining-room and old Arthur in the hall. We have our special table, and when a tragedy occurs we look the other way because it's the thing to do.

MILLY. You are very confused. Cynthia. Please let us take you to your room.

CYNTHIA. The limbless lie on the streets. Flesh spatters the car parks. 'Brits Out' it says on a rock-face, and we smile as we drive by. (*Pause.*)

For months he searched for her, pushing his way among the people of Birmingham and London, the people who were her victims. Endlessly he found her trail, endlessly he lost it again. While day by day she sat in Maida Vale, putting together the mechanisms of her bombs.

DEKKO. Bombs?

STRAFE. Cynthia, we've been very patient with you, but really this is just becoming silly.

CYNTHIA. Someone had told him about her. Someone had mentioned her name, and he couldn't believe it. This girl who had laughed on the seashore, whom he had loved and remembered still with love. Whenever he heard of bombs exploding he thought of her, and couldn't understand. He wept when he said that; her violence haunted him, he said.

STRAFE (*angrily*). Cynthia, will you kindly keep your voice down?

CYNTHIA. He couldn't work, he couldn't sleep at night. His mind filled up with images of her, their awkward childhood kisses, her fingers working neatly now with fuses. He saw her with a carrier-bag, hurrying it through a crowd, leaving it somewhere. In front of the mouldering old house that had once been Glencorn Lodge they made a fire and cooked their food. They lay for ages on the grass, they cycled home in the dark.

Hold sound effects under.

MILLY (*as narrator*). It suddenly dawned on me that Cynthia was knitting this whole fantasy out of nothing. It all worked backwards from the moment when she'd had the misfortune to witness the man's death in the sea. A few minutes before he'd been chatting quite normally to her, he'd probably even mentioned a holiday in his childhood and some girl there'd been: all of it would have been natural in the circumstances, possibly even the holiday had taken place at Glencorn. He'd said good-bye and then unfortunately he'd had his accident. Watching from the cliff edge, something had cracked in poor Cynthia's brain, she having always been a prey to melancholy. I suppose it must be hard having two sons who don't think much of you, and a marriage not offering you a great deal, bridge and holidays the best part of it probably. For some odd reason of her own she'd had a fantasy about a child turning into a terrorist. The violence of the man's death had clearly filled her imagination with Irish violence, so regularly seen on television. If we'd been on holiday in Suffolk I wondered how it would all have seemed to the poor creature. I could feel Strafe and Dekko beginning to put all that together also, beginning to realise that the whole story of the red-haired man and the girl was clearly Cynthia's invention. 'Poor creature', I wanted to say, but did not do so.

Sound effects: continue scene.

CYNTHIA. When he found her she just looked at him, as if the past hadn't even existed. She didn't smile, as if incapable of smiling. He wanted to take her away, back to where they came from, but she didn't even reply when he suggested that. Bitterness was like a disease in her, and when he left her he felt the bitterness in himself. (*Pause.*) He remained in London, working on the railways, but in the same way as before he was haunted by the person she'd become, and the haunting was more awful now. He bought a gun from a man he'd been told about and kept it hidden in a shoe-box in his rented room. Now and again he took it out and looked at it, then put it back. He hated the violence that possessed her, yet already he was full of it himself: he knew he couldn't betray her with anything but death. Humanity had left both of them when he visited her again in Maida Vale.

STRAFE (*very quietly*). The Malseeds are coming to have a word, dear. Please try to control yourself now.

MR *and* MRS MALSEED *arrive at the table.* MR MALSEED *speaks in an equally quiet voice.*

MALSEED. I must apologise, Mrs Strafe. I cannot say how sorry we are that you were bothered by that man.

MRS MALSEED. We hope you're quite recovered now, Mrs Strafe.

STRAFE. My wife is still a little dicky. But after a decent night's rest I think we can say she'll be as right as rain again.

MALSEED. I only wish, Mrs Strafe, you had made contact with Mrs Malseed or myself when he first approached you. I mean, the unpleasantness you suffered might just have been averted.

CYNTHIA. Nothing would have been averted, and certainly not the horror we are left with.

MALSEED. I'm afraid you've rather lost me, Mrs Strafe.

CYNTHIA. That man told me a story about two children who once were happy here and then became two murderers.

MALSEED. Oh now, I'm sure that's not quite so.

STRAFE. My wife —

CYNTHIA. Was I wrong to assume she had a wretched home? There's nothing to suggest her parents quarrelled, but don't you see why I thought of it? There must be some reason, some kind of explanation, I thought.

MRS MALSEED (*a laugh in her voice*). We really are a bit at sea, you know.

STRAFE (*laughing rather unpleasantly*). Yes I'm afraid we all are.

CYNTHIA. She sat at a chipped white table, her wires and fuses spread around her. In a back street he bought his gun for too much money. When did it first occur to him to kill her?

MALSEED (*very firmly*). We don't know these people, Mrs Strafe.

CYNTHIA. What were her thoughts in that room Mr Malseed? What happens in the mind of anyone who wishes to destroy?

MALSEED. That is something I have no desire to know.

CYNTHIA. Why not, Mr Malseed? Don't you think we should root our heads out of the sand and wonder, just once in a while? What is the truth about people who are so far beyond the Pale?

STRAFE. My dear, Mr Malseed is a busy man.

MRS MALSEED. There is unrest here, Mrs Strafe, but we do our best to live with it.

STRAFE. Of course.

CYNTHIA. And our stomachs turn when we consider those who cause it. Yet we are one with them.

MALSEED. Most emphatically, Mrs Strafe, neither my wife nor I is that. The tragedy is done with. I only wish it might have occurred elsewhere. If you're asking us to be sympathetic towards violent people we cannot help you.

CYNTHIA. I'm asking you if there can be regret that two children end like this.

MALSEED (angrily). I'm sorry, I simply don't see where children come into it.

CYNTHIA. Then I must begin again at the very beginning.

STRAFE. Absolutely not. The Malseeds don't wish to hear all this, you know.

CYNTHIA. Two children we hardly know about happened by chance to be in love. They sat in the long grass in front of a ruined house, they grew up with a sense of history that's natural in this island —

MALSEED. I beg you, Mrs Strafe, no politics in Glencorn Lodge.

CYNTHIA. Are they victims of politics, and of history too: is that it? Of loud-mouthed clergymen and grim idealists, all of them beyond the Pale we talk about? England has always had its Pales. Did you know that, Mrs Malseed? The one in Ireland began in 1395.

MILLY. Dear, I think Mr Malseed is perfectly right. This has nothing to do with calling people murderers and placing them beyond some Pale or other. You witnessed a most unpleasant accident, dear, and it's only to be expected that you've become just a little confused. The man had a chat with you while you were sitting among the shrubs and then the shock of seeing him slip on the seaweed —

CYNTHIA (screams her interruption). My God, he didn't slip on the seaweed!

STRAFE (almost as loudly as CYNTHIA). Cynthia, stop this immediately.

The tea lounge has become silent again.

MALSEED. I must ask you to take Mrs Strafe to her room, Major. And really we cannot tolerate further upsets in Glencorn Lodge.

STRAFE (*quietly*). Come along now.

CYNTHIA (*speaks much more quietly also*). An unbecoming tale, of course it can't be true. It's just an Irish joke that a man spent a night in a room called Japonica, in the vain hope that if he walked again by the seashore and through the woods he might somehow understand where a woman's cruelty had come from.

MALSEED. This talk is most offensive. You are trying to bring something to our doorstep which most certainly does not belong there.

MRS MALSEED (*gently*). Come along now, Mrs Strafe. Just to please us, dear. Kitty wants to clear away the tea things. (*She calls out.*) Yes please, Kitty.

When CYNTHIA *speaks she does so very calmly, quite in charge of herself again.*

CYNTHIA. I don't need to go to my room. If I may, I'll have a cup of tea.

MILLY. Oh, good.

CYNTHIA *picks up her cup and saucer.* KITTY *arrives with her tray.*

MRS MALSEED. Mrs Strafe won't be a moment, Kitty.

CYNTHIA. Yes, please do clear away.

She has become the CYNTHIA *of the night before, her voice a little sad, certainly humble.* KITTY *begins to clear away. The* MALSEEDS *are about to move off, though hesitating in case there's further trouble.*

CYNTHIA. What do you think of us, Kitty?

KITTY. Ma'am?

STRAFE. Cynthia . . .

MRS MALSEED. I think, dear, Kitty's quite busy really —

CYNTHIA. For fourteen years you've served us with food and cleared away the tea-cups we've drunk from. For fourteen years we've played our bridge and walked about the garden. We've gone for drives, we've bought our bits of tweed, we've bathed as those children did.

KITTY. Ach sure you're always welcome at Glencorn Ma'am.

STRAFE (*furiously*). Stop this at once, Cynthia.

MILLY (*as narrator*). But even as he spoke I made a sign at him because for some reason I felt that the end really was in sight.

CYNTHIA. In Surrey we while away the time, we clip our hedges. On bridge nights there's coffee at nine o'clock, with macaroons or petits fours. Last thing of all we watch the late-night news, packing away our cards and scoring-pads, our sharpened pencils. There's been an incident

in Armargh, one soldier's had his head shot off, another's run amok.
Our lovely Glens of Antrim, we all four think, our coastal drives: we
hope that nothing disturbs the peace. We think of Mr Malseed, still
busy in Glencorn Lodge and Mrs Malseed finishing her flower plaques
for the doors of the completed annexe.

KITTY. They're nice all right, the little signs Mrs Malseed does . . . I
often said that to her Ma'am.

CYNTHIA. Through honey-tinted glasses we love you and your island,
Kitty, the memory of your kings and high-kings, your earls and heroes.

STRAFE's *patience snaps. He shouts explosively at his wife.*

STRAFE. Will you for God's sake, shut up? You're a bloody spectacle
if you want to know, sitting there with your rubbish.

CYNTHIA. We love the lilt of your racy history, the marvels of your
landscape. Yet it was a sensible Pale we made here once, as civilised
people create a garden, pretty as a picture.

STRAFE (*quietly*). I'm sorry, dear. Sorry. But we honestly don't want
to hear any more about a Pale.

MRS MALSEED (*whispering*). As quickly as you can now, Kitty.

The further rattle of tea cups etc as KITTY *hastens.*

STRAFE (*whispering*). Pull yourself together, dear. Forget about this
Pale thing.

CYNTHIA. Beyond it lie the bleak untouchables, best kept as dots on
the horizon, too terrible to contemplate. How can we be blamed if
we make neither head nor tail of anything, we people of Surrey? Your
past and your present, Kitty, those battles and acts of parliament:
(*Pause.*) how can we know?

KITTY. Ach now, ma'am, why would you be bothering your head over
things like that?

Pause.

CYNTHIA. Yet I stupidly thought, you see, that the tragedy of two
children could at least be understood. He didn't discover where her
cruelty had come from because perhaps you never can: evil breeds
evil in a mysterious way. That's the story the red-haired stranger
passed on to me, Mr Malseed, the story we huddle away from.

MALSEED. Mrs Strafe —

CYNTHIA. That woman sitting there, Kitty, looking so concerned, is
my husband's mistress, a fact I'm supposed to be unaware of.

STRAFE. My God!

MILLY. For God's sake, Cynthia.

CYNTHIA. My husband is perverted in his sexual desires. His friend, who shared his schooldays, has never quite recovered from that time. I myself am a pathetic creature who has closed her eyes to a husband's infidelity and his mistress's viciousness. I am dragged down Memory Lane, back to the days of Thrive Major and A.D. Cowley-Stubbs: mechanically I smile. I hardly exist, Kitty.

KITTY. Ach, you exist all right ma'am . . . only I think . . .

STRAFE (*shouting*). Oh, for God's sake, Cynthia, go and rest yourself.

CYNTHIA. I've had a rest. But it didn't do any good because hell has invaded the paradise of Glencorn, Kitty, as it has so often invaded your island. And we, who have so often brought it, pretend it isn't there. Who cares about children made into murderers?

STRAFE (*furiously*). You fleshless bitch. You awful, fleshless bitch.

Silence.

CYNTHIA. No one cares, Kitty, and on our journey home we shall all four be silent. Yet is the truth about ourselves at least a beginning? Shall we wonder in the end about the hell that frightens us?

MILLY *is furious by now. She speaks with great anger, her tears constantly threatening.*

Hold sound effects under.

MILLY (*as narrator*). Strafe had closed his eyes in misery and I wanted to reach out and take his hand, but of course I could not. The Malseeds were clearly under the impression that what they'd just heard was more of Cynthia's fantasy, but for us that could not be so. Everything was suddenly different because of what she'd said, everything was ruined. I wanted to shout at her too, to batter the silliness out of her, but of course I could not do that either. I could feel the tears behind my eyes and I couldn't help noticing that Dekko's hands were shaking. He's quite sensitive behind his joky manner, and had obviously taken to heart her statement that he had never grown up. Nor had it been pleasant, hearing myself described as vicious. I wanted to reach out and hurt her.

Bring up the sound of the tea things being collected, and the other sounds of the tea lounge.

She stumbled off eventually and none of us followed her. I knew she was right when she said we would just go home, away from this country we had come to love. And I knew as well that neither here nor at home would she be led into a blue van because that would be too easy an end for all of us. Strafe would stay with her because Strafe is honourable, and when I thought of that I felt a pain where my heart is and again I wanted to cry. Why couldn't it have been she who had gone down to the rocks and slipped on the seaweed or just walked into the sea, it didn't matter which? Her awful rigmarole hung about us as the last of the tea things were gathered up, the earls who'd fled, the famines and the people planted. The children were there too, grown up into murdering riff-raff.

Bring up, during this speech, the sound of the sea. It begins as a soft lapping as waves break over sand. As it becomes louder it also becomes more agitated until, after MILLY's voice has ceased, it is a roar of waves crashing through rocks. It ceases abruptly.